Betty Crocker

COMPLETE

Thanksgiving
COOKBOOK

All You Need to Cook a Foolproof Dinner

WILEY

Wiley Publishing, Inc.

GENERAL MILLS, INC.

Director, Books and Electronic Publishing:
Kim Walter

Manager, Books: Lois L. Tlusty

Editor: Cheri A. Olerud

Recipe Development and Testing: Betty Crocker Kitchens

Food Styling: Betty Crocker Kitchens

Photography: General Mills Photo Studios

WILEY PUBLISHING, INC.

Publisher: Natalie Chapman

Executive Editor: Anne Ficklen

Editor: Caroline Schleifer

Production Editor: Donna Wright

Cover Design: Edwin Kuo and Holly Wittenberg

Interior Design: Sandy St. Jacques and
Holly Wittenberg

Interior Layout: Holly Wittenberg

Interior Illustrations: Adam Raiti

Manufacturing Buyer: Kevin Watt

Our Betty Crocker Kitchens seal guarantees success in your kitchen. Every recipe has been tested in America's Most Trusted Kitchens™ to meet our high standards of reliability, easy preparation and great taste.

Manufactured in the United States

10 9 8 7 6 5 4 3 2

Cover photo: Grilled Lemon-Herb Turkey (page 26).

For more great ideas visit **www.bettycrocker.com**

For general information on our other products and services or to obtain technical support please contact our Customer Care Department within the U.S. at 800-762-2974, outside the U.S. at 317-572-3993 or fax 317-572-4002.

Wiley also publishes its books in a variety of electronic formats. Some content that appears in print may not be available in electronic books.

Library of Congress Cataloging-in-Publication Data:
Crocker, Betty.
  [Complete Thanksgiving Cookbook]
  Betty Crocker Complete Thanksgiving cookbook : all you need to cook a foolproof dinner—1st ed.
      p. cm.
Includes index.
   ISBN 0-7645-2574-3
   1. Thanksgiving cookery. 2. Menus. I. Title: Complete Thanksgiving cookbook. II. Title.
   TX739.2.T45C76 2003
641.5'68—dc21
                                                          2003008728

Dear Friends,

Thanksgiving . . . the very thought of it evokes rich aromas and the warm, cozy memories of mother, grandmother or another favorite relative cooking a delicious feast for the whole family. Or of neighbors gathering to share a festive meal, full of fellowship and fun. Now you can create those same happy moments with help from Betty Crocker. Whether you're cooking Thanksgiving dinner for the first time or have hosted this dinner for years, you'll find all you need to make your holiday special in *Betty Crocker Complete Thanksgiving Cookbook.*

Now that it's your turn to create the traditions that you'll pass along, you may wonder how Mom or Grandma always made it all so tasty. How did they roast a turkey that was beautifully golden, or make such smooth, rich gravy? And how did they bake all the pies—from apple to pecan to pumpkin—you remember so well?

Thanksgiving is all about tradition—but the traditions that count the most are the ones that *you* cherish. In this cookbook, you'll find a whole range of recipes, from classics that you may have grown up with to new twists on the traditional. All the basics are here, step-by-step in "*Betty's Thank Goodness Advice*" pages, such as how to roast a turkey, make lump-free gravy, or roll out pie dough. And if you're in the mood to try something different, there are exciting new methods—like brining, smoking or grilling your turkey—to check out.

Thanksgiving can be the most challenging meal to prepare—even for the most experienced cooks. And if you've never made Thanksgiving dinner before, the idea can be daunting! There's no need to worry—the truth is, anyone can successfully prepare a delicious Thanksgiving dinner. Betty Crocker can walk you through all the steps with recipes, menus and easy-to-follow explanations that help you create the feast you've always wanted.

Betty Crocker

P.S. Thankfully, with a little help from Betty Crocker, Thanksgiving can be a memorable meal for family and friends—and for the cook as well!

Contents

You Asked Us

Thanksgiving can be a wonderful occasion to gather family and friends around the table for a celebration feast—or it can be a time of panic for first-time or even experienced cooks. Every year, during the weeks before the holiday, the Betty Crocker phone lines and Web site are flooded with questions from home cooks just like you. In fact, that was the reason this Thanksgiving survival cookbook was created—to help make your holiday hassle-free!

Rest assured! Answers to all of your Thanksgiving questions, recipe requests and more are included here. Then, turn the pages to discover chapters filled with everything you need to know: from the basics of preparing favorite Thanksgiving foods to delicious classic recipes as well as plenty of traditional recipes with a "twist" that you may want to try. You'll be able to concentrate on giving thanks when your dinner preparations are under control.

Your Questions Answered

Q. Talking Turkey

How do I select a turkey? What size turkey should I buy? How do I thaw a turkey? How do I prepare a turkey? How long can I keep a frozen turkey in my freezer? How can I make sure that my turkey is moist?

A. *It's Turkey Time*

If you've never prepared a turkey, you're bound to have lots of questions. Even if you've roasted plenty of turkeys before, you may still wonder how to ensure that your bird will turn out moist, flavorful and golden brown every time. Turkey Talk (page 14) answers all your turkey questions and more with top tips plus the how-to's of selecting, thawing, stuffing, roasting and carving, that walk you through every step. Just in case your family's favorite dinner isn't turkey and fixins', or if you want to serve another main dish, there's a whole chapter of More Great Main Dishes, (pages 90–107), for festive alternatives.

Q. Pie in the Sky

I've never made pastry before—is it hard to roll? Can I use pumpkin from my garden to make pumpkin pie? Can I make pumpkin pie without a crust? Do you have a really easy pie recipe? I remember a recipe for pumpkin pie that forms its own crust—how can I find that recipe?

A. *Bake Some Goodness*

What's more American than apple—or pumpkin, pecan, squash, sweet potato or pear for that matter—pie? Turn to the Delicious Desserts chapter for countless pies and variations, including Impossibly Easy Pumpkin Pie (page 157) made with Bisquick® mix. A pie primer, Blue Ribbon Pies (page 148), gives you easy, step-by-step instructions, particularly helpful if you're new to pie baking. There's a really easy pastry recipe, Pat-in-the-Pan Pastry (page 159), for a no-roll crust. Plenty of other desserts, from puddings and crisps to cakes, cookies and bars are included in the Delicious Desserts chapter as well.

Your Questions Answered

Q. Gravy Jitters

Making gravy makes me nervous—how do I make gravy without lumps? My gravy always gets too thick—what can I do? I'm deep-fat frying (or grilling) my turkey this year and won't have turkey drippings—how can I make tasty gravy? Do you have a recipe for gravy made with milk?

A. *Let It Pour*

First thing, consult Betty's Thank Goodness Advice for Great Gravy (page 46), for foolproof instructions on making smooth, lump-free gravy. It's complete with quick fix Gravy Rx's (page 47) to help with any last-minute problems. For fryer and grill fans, there's flavorful No-Drippings Gravy (page 49), using chicken broth. Recipes for several types of gravies, including Milk Gravy (page 50), are included in Chapter 2, Gravy, Stuffing and Sauces.

Q. New Cook Help

My in-laws are coming for Thanksgiving dinner, and I've never even prepared a chicken, not to mention a turkey—what should I do? Do you have ideas and recipes for new cooks who've never prepared Thanksgiving dinner? Where do I start first?

A. *First Feast*

Preparing your first Thanksgiving dinner for family or friends can be scary and perhaps a little intimidating. To help you plan your menu and determine what to cook when, turn to the special menu section for great ideas. You can choose from a Super-Simple Menu for 4 to 8 (page 180) that helps you with suggestions for what you can purchase instead of making yourself, or try out My First Thanksgiving Dinner for 8 menu (page 182), complete with a timing countdown, that walks you through every step of a traditional meal. Make sure to look over the different "Betty's Thank Goodness Advice" pages for detailed step-by-step explanations and tips on all the basics—from choosing the best wine to accompany your dinner (page 93) to rolling out pastry like a pro (page 148) and lots more.

Do-Ahead, Plan and Organize

How can I get everything done at the same time? What dishes can I prepare ahead of time and how should I store them? What's the best way to reheat a dish I've prepared ahead? Can I bake rolls ahead of time? How do I freeze them? I've only got one oven, how can I cook everything?

Make a List and Check It Twice

Though Thanksgiving is only one day, anyone who has successfully prepared Thanksgiving dinner knows that planning and preparation starts weeks (or at least days) in advance. First, look through this book and plan your menu. As you select recipes, look for a special tip, called Betty's Do-Ahead, that tells you what you can get done ahead of time. Write down your menu and the number of guests, then get all your recipes out, check your ingredients and make a list of the foods you will need to buy. The day before Thanksgiving, you can set the table and plan which serving platters and utensils, bowls and baskets you'll need. If you have only one oven, it's likely that the turkey will be taking up most of your heating space. Make sure to choose side dishes that can be prepared on the stovetop; use your toaster oven to reheat rolls; warm vegetables in the microwave; and be sure to use your slow cooker for stuffing or other sides. Or consider an alternate cooking method like grilling or deep-frying for the turkey to free up your oven for the sides.

 New Ways with the Bird

Everyone is talking about deep-fat frying turkeys—how do you do it? I saw a TV demonstration on high-heat roasting a turkey—can turkey really be roasted at that high temperature and stay moist? My family wants to grill the turkey this year—is that even possible? Are self-basting turkeys a good bet?

Terrific New Techniques

A fun way to start a new family tradition is to try a new way of cooking the versatile turkey. Grilling (page 26) and deep-fat frying (page 27) have recently become popular methods, especially in warmer climes, where cooking outdoors in November remains a pleasant possibility. There are many other successful methods to check out, including high-heat roasting (page 25); smoking (page 31); or brining (page 33). Or cook the self-basting turkeys that virtually guarantee moist and tender meat.

Your Questions Answered

Q. **Over the River and Through the Woods**

I'm looking for a side dish (or dessert) that can travel. I need to take my favorite green bean casserole on a 4-hour car trip—how can I pack it to go that far? How do I heat it once I get there?

A. *Foods that are Good to Go*

Even if you're not in charge of the whole meal this year, you may want to bring a favorite food or the host may ask you to bring your signature dish. If you're hosting the meal, some of your guests may enjoy bringing something special to share. Whether you're going across the street or to the next state, it's just a matter of choosing the best kinds of foods to take on the road. In general, it's a good idea if the host prepares the star of the meal—the turkey. For food safety reasons and because they can be cumbersome to wrap and pack, turkey and other main dishes (except casseroles), stuffing and gravy, and refrigerated or cream pies are not terrific travelers. But there are plenty of other great dishes that are good to go! Check out the top tips in Make and Take (page 135) for foods that travel well. Remember your slow cooker when you want to bring something warm—as long as you plug it in within the hour, it's a great way to tote.

Q. **Health Concerns**

What can I make for a vegetarian friend for Thanksgiving dinner? We just learned that my father has diabetes. He loves Thanksgiving—how will I make a meal for him that follows his food plan? I'm on a low-fat diet—what can I make for Thanksgiving dinner?

A. *Healthy and Happy*

Health concerns can make it more tricky, of course, but not impossible to plan what to cook and serve for Thanksgiving. Fortunately for your guests, one of the pleasures of Thanksgiving is having a whole range of favorite dishes to choose from. If you have just one vegetarian guest, it's likely that he or she will be happy choosing from the wonderful side dishes you make and will just skip the turkey. However, if friends or family members are planning to go meatless this year, you can try the Vegetarian Thanksgiving Dinner menu (page 131) that packs in traditional flavor without the meat To learn more about cooking for someone with diabetes, turn to the Delicious Diabetes Dinner menu (page 80) that suggests serving plenty of fresh vegetable side dishes that everyone will enjoy. Anyone looking for healthful choices will be pleased to try the delicious options in the Low-Fat Thanksgiving Dinner menu (page 78) that's fully satisfying.

Q. Quantity with Quality

How in the world can I prepare Thanksgiving dinner for my family of 25? I'm volunteering at a homeless shelter (or church or community center) this year for Thanksgiving—any ideas for preparing a meal for 40?

A. *Crowd-Control*

One of the best aspects of Thanksgiving is sharing the meal with others, so the more the merrier! But it does require lots of organizing and planning to pull off a great meal for a crowd. If you're up to the challenge, turn first to the basic tips, menu and countdown that are included in the Thanksgiving Dinner for a Crowd menu (page 183). Delegating is one of the best ways to get it all done, so ask for help—whether it's preparing some of the side dishes, bringing dessert, setting the table(s), serving or cleaning up. When everyone pitches in, including kids, the true spirit of Thanksgiving really shines.

Q. Leftover Mania

I cooked way too much! What can I do with all the leftover turkey, stuffing and gravy? Do you have any recipes for using up all this food?

A. *Lucky You with Leftovers*

One of the best things about Thanksgiving is all the delicious leftovers! There's so much more than turkey sandwiches to enjoy the next day—check out recipes for Homemade Turkey Soup (page 38), Turkey and Stuffing Casserole (page 40), and Cranberry-Turkey Salad (page 42), among others, in the Turkey Encores section of Chapter 1 (pages 12–43).

Most Requested Recipes

Many favorite recipes are asked for over and over at Thanksgiving time. Some of the oldest and simplest American recipes are the most treasured. Not surprisingly, many of these recipes are the same as the classic (or traditional) recipes that have been passed down from generation to generation. Here are the recipes that are most frequently requested from Betty Crocker. You may find they're your family's favorites too!

- **Sausage-Cheese Balls** (page 126)
- **Bountiful Twice-Baked Potatoes** (page 74)
- *Classic* **Sweet Potatoes with Marshmallows** (page 75)
- *Classic* **Baked Corn Pudding** (page 83)
- *Classic* **Green Bean Casserole** (page 69)
- *Classic* **Dinner Rolls** (page 112)
- *Classic* **Pumpkin Pie** (page 154)
- **Impossibly Easy Pumpkin Pie** (page 157)
- *Classic* **Apple Pie** (page 161)

Turkey Tribute *and* Encores

Turkey Talk

The favorite part of any holiday feast deserves to be treated right! No matter how you decide to serve up this noble bird, here are some great tips and techniques to help you prepare the perfect turkey.

Selecting Your Turkey

Whole ready-to-cook turkeys can range in size from 8 to 24 pounds. How much should you buy? Whether it's your first turkey or your tenth, that's always the question! Allow about 1 pound of uncooked whole turkey per person. That makes enough for a feast, as well as leftovers. Choose a turkey that is plump and meaty with smooth, moist-looking skin. The skin should be creamy colored. The cut ends of the bones should be pink to red in color.

There's no difference in quality between fresh and frozen turkey. Keep fresh whole turkeys refrigerated and cook them within 1 to 2 days of buying. Store whole frozen turkeys in your freezer at 0° for up to 6 months. These recipes were tested with prebasted turkeys as well as fresh and frozen, and we found there was no difference, so use whatever kind you prefer.

Thawing Your Turkey

There are three safe ways to thaw a frozen turkey. Thawing at room temperature is not recommended since it promotes bacterial growth.

1 Gradual Thaw in Refrigerator

This is the preferred method. Refrigerate frozen turkey (in original packaging) on a tray to collect liquids. Allow about 24 hours per 5 pounds of whole turkey. An 8- to 12-pound turkey will thaw in about 2 days.

2 Gradual Thaw in Cold Water

If you need to thaw a turkey more quickly, choose this method. Leave the turkey in its original packaging, free from tears or holes. Place in a sink or large clean container filled with cold water, and change the water often. Allow about 30 minutes per pound for whole turkeys. An 8- to 12-pound turkey will thaw in about 5 hours.

3 Quick Thaw in Microwave

If you need to thaw a turkey even faster, choose this method. Remove all packaging from turkey and place in a large, microwave-safe container. Leave uncovered. Thaw turkey in the microwave following the microwave manufacturer's directions.

Turkey Thawing Timetable

Plan ahead if you buy a frozen turkey. Large turkeys will need several days to thaw in the refrigerator. Once thawed, the turkey may be refrigerated up to 2 days before roasting.

Approximate Weight (pounds)	Thawing Time in Refrigerator
8 to 12	1 to 2 days
12 to 16	2 to 3 days
16 to 20	3 to 4 days
20 to 24	4 to 5 days

Preparing Your Turkey

While the oven heats, prepare the turkey for roasting. Stuff the turkey just before cooking. This will prevent bacteria from contaminating the stuffing. Never prestuff a turkey and refrigerate or freeze for later roasting.

1 Remove outer wrapping from turkey. Remove package of giblets (gizzard, heart, liver and neck) from neck cavity of turkey and discard. (If making Giblet Stock, page 21, place giblets in saucepan and add other ingredients.)

2 Rinse neck and body cavities with cool water; pat dry with paper towels. Rub both cavities lightly with salt if desired, but do not salt cavities if stuffing the turkey.

3 Stuff turkey, packing stuffing loosely (stuffing expands while it bakes) into the neck cavity. Then, fasten neck skin to the back with skewers, and fold wings across the back with the tips touching. Next, loosely fill the body cavity. Tuck the drumsticks under the band of skin at the tail (or tie or skewer to the tail).

4 If not stuffing turkey, fasten neck skin to back of turkey with skewer. Fold wings across back of turkey so tips are touching. Place seasonings in body cavity.

Top Turkey Tips

- **Quantity:** When figuring what size turkey to buy, allow about 1 pound per person. The amount of sliced, cooked turkey is about 50 percent of the weight of a whole turkey.

- **Tenderness:** Generally, the younger the turkey, the more tender the meat will be. Turkeys available today will usually be labeled "young," meaning 4 to 6 months old.

- **Timing:** Make sure you start with a fully thawed turkey. Cooking charts are based on thawed turkeys, and the time and doneness can vary greatly if the turkey is still partially frozen.

- **Moistness:** For the juiciest bird possible, don't overcook it. Use a meat thermometer to test for doneness. The internal temperature should reach 180° for whole birds and 170° for whole turkey breasts and bone-in or boneless pieces.

- **Extra Help:** You can contact the USDA Meat and Poultry Hotline at 800-535-4555 or Web site at www.fsis.usda.gov/OA/programs/mphotlin.htm; Butterball Turkey Talk Line at 800-323-4848 or Web site at www.butterball.com; or Reynolds Kitchens Turkey Tips Line at 800-745-4000 or Web site at www.reynoldskitchens.com. And for all kinds of Thanksgiving help and other great ideas, check out www.BettyCrocker.com.

continues

Roasting Your Turkey

Roasting your turkey may actually be the easiest part of your meal. For golden brown skin and moist, tender meat, roast your turkey at a medium temperature (325°) according to the Turkey Roasting Timetable (below). For an equally tender and delicious turkey, you can roast at a high temperature (450°), instead, following the timetable for high-heat roasting. (For complete high-heat roasting directions, see page 25.)

1 Place turkey, breast side up, on a rack in a shallow roasting pan. Brush with melted butter, margarine or oil. If using an ovenproof meat thermometer, place it so the tip is in the thickest part of the inside thigh muscle and does not touch bone. (Do not add water or cover turkey.)

2 When two-thirds through the roasting time, cut the band of skin at the tail, or remove the skewer or tie holding the drumsticks together, to allow inside of thighs to cook through.

3 Begin checking turkey doneness about 1 hour before end of recommended roasting time. Turkey is done when thermometer reads 180° and juice of turkey is no longer pink when you cut into center of thigh. The drumstick should move easily when lifted or twisted. Thermometer placed in center of stuffing will read 165° when done. If the turkey has turned golden brown but is not done, place a tent of aluminum foil loosely over the turkey if desired.

4 When the turkey is done, transfer it, breast side up, to a carving board and let stand, loosely covered with foil, 15 to 20 minutes. Cutting the turkey will be easier and slices will be uniform if turkey stands before carving.

Roasting Turkey Timetable

Follow this timetable for regular roasting or high-heat roasting. For prestuffed turkeys, follow package directions very carefully—do not use this timetable.

Ready-to-Cook Weight (pounds)	Approximate Roasting Time at 325° (hours)	High-Heat Roasting Time at 450° (hours)
Whole Turkey (stuffed)		
8 to 12	3 to 3 1/2	Not recommended
12 to 14	3 1/2 to 4	
14 to 18	4 to 4 1/4	
18 to 20	4 1/4 to 4 3/4	
20 to 24	4 3/4 to 5 1/4	
Whole Turkey (not stuffed)		
8 to 12	2 3/4 to 3	45 minutes to 1 1/4
12 to 14	3 to 3 3/4	
14 to 18	3 3/4 to 4 1/4	1 1/2 to 1 3/4
18 to 20	4 1/4 to 4 1/2	
20 to 24	4 1/2 to 5	2 3/4 to 3 1/4
Turkey Breast (bone-in)		
2 to 4	1 1/2 to 2	Not recommended
3 to 5	1 1/2 to 2 1/2	
5 to 7	2 to 2 1/2	

Carving Your Turkey

To begin, place the turkey, breast side up and with its legs to your right if you're right-handed or to the left if left-handed. Remove skewers or ties. Remove stuffing from the bird before carving and put it in a separate serving dish or container.

1 While gently pulling the leg and thigh away from the body, cut through the joint between leg and body. Separate the drumstick (leg) and thigh by cutting down through the connecting joint. Serve the drumstick and thighs whole, or carve them. To carve, remove meat from drumstick by slicing at an angle, and slice thigh by cutting even slices parallel to the bone.

2 Make a deep horizontal cut into the breast just above the wing.

3 Insert fork in the top of the breast, and starting halfway up the breast, carve thin slices down to the horizontal cut, working from outer edge of bird to the center. Repeat steps on the other side of the turkey.

Top Carving Tips

- Carving is easier and slices will be more uniform if the turkey is allowed to stand for about 15 minutes after roasting.

- Use a sharp carving knife and a meat fork for best results—safely—when carving. A carving knife that has a long, curved blade works best. A meat fork has a long handle and two tines.

- Carve on a stable cutting surface, such as a cutting board, meat carving board or platter, to catch the juices.

- If you aren't serving the turkey immediately, cover with aluminum foil to keep warm, and serve within 10 minutes.

1

Separate the drumstick and thigh by cutting through the connecting joint.

3

Carve thin slices down the horizontal cut.

2

Make a horizontal cut in the breast above the wing.

Classic Roast Turkey

Prep: 25 min   **Roast:** 3 hr 30 min   **Stand:** 15 min   **8 to 12 servings**

8- to 12-pound turkey, thawed if frozen

Classic Bread Stuffing (page 52), if desired

2 tablespoons butter or margarine, melted

1 Heat oven to 325°. Prepare turkey for roasting as directed on page 15.

2 Make Classic Bread Stuffing. Stuff turkey just before roasting, not ahead of time. Fill neck cavity lightly with stuffing. Fasten neck skin to back of turkey with skewer. Fold wings across back of turkey so tips are touching. Fill body cavity lightly with stuffing. (Do not pack stuffing because it will expand during roasting.) Tuck drumsticks under band of skin at tail, or tie together with heavy string, then tie to tail.

3 Place turkey, breast side up, on rack in shallow roasting pan. Brush butter over turkey. Insert ovenproof meat thermometer so tip is in thickest part of inside thigh muscle and does not touch bone. (Do not add water or cover turkey.)

4 Roast uncovered 3 hours to 3 hours 30 minutes. After about 2 hours, when turkey begins to turn golden, cut band of skin or remove tie holding drumsticks to allow inside of thighs to cook through, then place a tent of aluminum foil loosely over turkey.

5 Turkey is done when thermometer reads 180° and juice of turkey is no longer pink when you cut into center of thigh. The drumstick should move easily when lifted or twisted. Thermometer placed in center of stuffing will read 165° when done. If a meat thermometer is not used, begin testing for doneness after about 2 hours 30 minutes. When turkey is done, place on warm platter and cover with aluminum foil to keep warm. Let stand about 15 minutes for easiest carving. Cover and refrigerate any remaining turkey and stuffing separately.

1 Serving: Calories 385 (Calories from Fat 205); Fat 23g (Saturated 6g); Cholesterol 140mg; Sodium 170mg; Carbohydrate 0g (Dietary Fiber 0g); Protein 44g. **Diet Exchanges:** 6 Lean Meat, 1 Fat.

Betty's Do-Ahead

Frozen turkey tastes just as good as fresh and is easily available at any supermarket. Just remember to allow extra time for thawing. To thaw a whole turkey, place turkey (in its original wrap) in a baking pan in the refrigerator for 2 to 3 days. (See page 14 for thawing instructions.)

Cranberry–Apple Glazed Turkey

Prep: 25 min   **Cook:** 10 min   **Roast:** 4 hr   **Stand:** 15 min   **18 to 20 servings**

(see photo insert)

12-pound turkey, thawed if frozen

Cranberry Stuffing (page 57)

2 tablespoons butter or margarine, melted

Cranberry-Apple Glaze (below)

1 Heat oven to 325°. Prepare turkey for roasting as directed on page 15.

2 Make Cranberry Stuffing. Stuff turkey just before roasting, not ahead of time. Fill neck cavity lightly with stuffing. Fasten neck skin to back of turkey with skewer. Fold wings across back of turkey so tips are touching. Fill body cavity lightly with stuffing. (Do not pack stuffing because it will expand during roasting.) Tuck drumsticks under band of skin at tail, or tie together with heavy string, then tie to tail.

3 Place turkey, breast side up, on rack in shallow roasting pan. Brush butter over turkey. Insert ovenproof meat thermometer so tip is in thickest part of inside thigh muscle and does not touch bone. (Do not add water or cover turkey.)

4 Roast uncovered 3 hours 30 minutes to 4 hours. After about 2 hours, when turkey begins to turn golden, cut band of skin or remove tie holding drumsticks to allow inside of thighs to cook through, then place a tent of aluminum foil loosely over turkey. While turkey is roasting, make Cranberry-Apple Glaze. Brush glaze on turkey about 20 minutes before turkey is done.

5 Turkey is done when thermometer reads 180° and juice of turkey is no longer pink when you cut into center of thigh. The drumstick should move easily when lifted or twisted. Thermometer placed in center of stuffing will read 165° when done. If a meat thermometer is not used, begin testing for doneness after about 3 hours. When turkey is done, place on warm platter and cover with aluminum foil to keep warm. Let stand about 15 minutes for easiest carving.

6 To serve, brush again with glaze before carving. Cover and refrigerate any remaining turkey and stuffing separately.

Betty's
Special Touch

If you have any unused Cranberry-Apple Glaze left over, save it for dessert! It makes a delicious fruity topping to drizzle over vanilla ice cream or pound cake.

1 Serving: Calories 425 (Calories from Fat 200); Fat 22g (Saturated 10g); Cholesterol 125mg; Sodium 440mg; Carbohydrate 23g (Dietary Fiber 1g); Protein 34g. **Diet Exchanges:** 1 1/2 Starch, 4 Lean Meat, 1 Fat.

Cranberry-Apple Glaze

1 can (8 ounces) jellied cranberry sauce

1/4 cup apple jelly

1/4 cup light corn syrup

Mix all ingredients in 1-quart saucepan. Cook over medium heat about 5 minutes, stirring occasionally, until melted and smooth.

Savory Apple-Onion Turkey

Prep: 40 min   **Roast:** 3 hr 30 min   **Stand:** 15 min   **15 to 18 servings**

12- to 14-pound turkey, thawed if frozen

2 teaspoons onion salt

3 slices thick-sliced bacon, cut in half

1 medium onion, cut into thin wedges

1 medium apple, cored and cut into eight pieces

2 tablespoons vegetable oil

Giblet Stock (next page), if desired

1 cup apple jelly

2 tablespoons Dijon mustard

Apple Cider Gravy (next page)

1 Heat oven to 325°. Prepare turkey for roasting as directed on page 15, reserving giblets to make Giblet Stock if desired.

2 Fasten neck skin to back of turkey with skewer. Fold wings across back of turkey so tips are touching. Sprinkle 1 teaspoon of the onion salt in cavity.

3 Place turkey, breast side up, on rack in shallow roasting pan. Starting at back opening of the turkey, gently separate skin from turkey breast, using fingers. Place half slices of bacon under the skin; secure skin at lower edge with toothpick or metal skewer. Place onion and apple in turkey cavity. Brush oil over turkey; sprinkle with remaining 1 teaspoon onion salt. Insert ovenproof meat thermometer so tip is in thickest part of inside thigh muscle and does not touch bone. (Do not add water or cover turkey.)

4 Roast uncovered 3 hours to 3 hours 30 minutes. While turkey is roasting, make Giblet Stock to use in gravy. After roasting about 2 hours, when it begins to turn golden, place a tent of aluminum foil loosely over turkey.

5 About 40 minutes before turkey is done, heat jelly and mustard to boiling in 1 1/2-quart saucepan; reduce heat. Simmer about 1 minute, stirring constantly, until jelly is melted. Set aside until turkey is almost done. Generously brush apple glaze over turkey frequently during last 30 minutes of roasting.

6 Turkey is done when thermometer reads 180° and juice of turkey is no longer pink when you cut into center of thigh. The drumstick should move easily when lifted or twisted. If a meat thermometer is not used, begin testing for doneness after about 2 hours 30 minutes. When turkey is done, place on warm platter and cover with aluminum foil to keep warm. Let stand about 15 minutes for easiest carving.

7 Make Apple Cider Gravy. Serve gravy with turkey. Cover and refrigerate any remaining turkey and gravy separately.

---

1 Serving: Calories 360 (Calories from Fat 135); Fat 15g (Saturated 4g); Cholesterol 110mg; Sodium 280mg; Carbohydrate 18g (Dietary Fiber 0g); Protein 38g. **Diet Exchanges:** 1 Starch, 5 Lean Meat.

Betty's Helpful Tip

Including the liver with the giblets in the Giblet Stock will give you a stronger-flavored stock and gravy. Discard the liver before cooking the stock if a milder-flavored gravy appeals to you more.

Giblet Stock

Reserved giblets and neck from turkey (see tip)

1 medium onion, cut into fourths

1/2 teaspoon onion salt

Place all ingredients in 3-quart saucepan; add enough water to cover. Heat to boiling; reduce heat to low. Cover and simmer 1 hour. Strain the stock through colander or wire strainer, discarding giblets, neck and onion. Refrigerate until needed to make gravy.

Apple Cider Gravy

About 1 1/2 cups Giblet Stock (above) or chicken broth

1 cup apple cider or apple wine

2/3 cup all-purpose flour

1/3 cup water

1/2 teaspoon salt

1/2 teaspoon pepper

Pour drippings (turkey juices and fat) from roasting pan into 4-cup measuring cup, leaving brown bits in pan. Add enough Giblet Stock to drippings to measure 3 cups; pour into 3-quart saucepan and set aside. Pour apple cider into roasting pan; cook over medium heat, stirring constantly, until all browned bits are released. Transfer cider mixture to liquid in 3-quart saucepan. Heat to boiling over medium-high heat. Beat flour and water in small bowl with wire whisk until well blended. Beat flour mixture into boiling liquid, using wire whisk; continue boiling and whisking 1 minute. Stir in salt and pepper.

Rosemary–Lemon Roasted Turkey

Prep: 10 min **Roast:** 4 hr **Stand:** 15 min **15 to 18 servings**

12- to 14-pound turkey, thawed if frozen

6 sprigs rosemary

3 lemons, cut into fourths

2 tablespoons vegetable oil

1 teaspoon garlic salt

1 Heat oven to 325°. Prepare turkey for roasting as directed on page 15.

2 Fasten neck skin to back of turkey with skewer. Fold wings across back of turkey so tips are touching. Place rosemary and lemon fourths in cavity of turkey.

3 Place turkey, breast side up, on rack in shallow roasting pan. Brush with oil. Sprinkle with garlic salt. Insert ovenproof meat thermometer so tip is in thickest part of inside thigh muscle and does not touch bone. (Do not add water or cover turkey.)

4 Roast uncovered 3 hours 30 minutes to 4 hours. After roasting about 2 hours, when turkey begins to turn golden, place a tent of aluminum foil loosely over turkey.

5 Turkey is done when thermometer reads 180° and juice of turkey is no longer pink when you cut into center of thigh. The drumstick should move easily when lifted or twisted. If a meat thermometer is not used, begin testing for doneness after about 3 hours. When turkey is done, place on warm platter and cover with aluminum foil to keep warm. Let stand about 15 minutes for easiest carving.

1 Serving: Calories 265 (Calories from Fat 115); Fat 13g (Saturated 4g); Cholesterol 105mg; Sodium 140mg; Carbohydrate 0g (Dietary Fiber 0g); Protein 37g. **Diet Exchanges:** 5 Lean Meat.

Betty's Special Touch

For a pretty presentation, garnish the turkey with fresh sprigs of rosemary and sage leaves. Add lemon wedges, red grapes and whole cranberries to the platter.

Southwestern Turkey

Prep: 20 min   **Roast:** 3 hr 45 min   **Stand:** 15 min   **15 to 18 servings**

12- to 14-pound turkey, thawed if frozen

8 to 10 fresh sage leaves

Slow Cooker Chorizo, Pecan and Cheddar Stuffing (page 56) or Classic Bread Stuffing (page 52), if desired

1/3 cup butter or margarine

1 teaspoon chili powder

1 teaspoon ground cumin

1 or 2 chipotle chilies in adobo sauce (from 7-ounce can), finely chopped

1 Heat oven to 325°. Prepare turkey for roasting as directed on page 15.

2 Starting at the back opening of the turkey, gently separate skin from turkey breast, using fingers. Place sage leaves under the skin.

3 Make one of the stuffings, but do not cook. Stuff turkey just before roasting, not ahead of time. Fill neck cavity lightly with stuffing. Fasten neck skin to back of turkey with skewer. Fold wings across back of turkey so tips are touching. Fill body cavity lightly with stuffing. (Do not pack stuffing because it will expand during roasting.) Tuck drumsticks under band of skin at tail, or tie together with heavy string, then tie to tail.

4 Place turkey, breast side up, on rack in shallow roasting pan. Heat butter, chili powder, cumin and chilies until butter is melted. Brush turkey with 2 tablespoons of the butter mixture. Insert ovenproof meat thermometer so tip is in the thickest part of inside thigh muscle and does not touch bone. (Do not add water or cover turkey.)

5 Roast uncovered 3 hours to 3 hours 45 minutes, brushing occasionally with remaining butter mixture. After roasting about 2 hours, place a tent of aluminum foil loosely over turkey when it begins to turn golden, and cut band of skin or remove tie holding drumsticks to allow inside of thighs to cook through.

6 Turkey is done when thermometer reads 180° and juice of turkey is no longer pink when you cut into center of thigh. The drumstick should move easily when lifted or twisted. Thermometer placed in center of stuffing will read 165° when done. If a meat thermometer is not used, begin testing for doneness after about 2 hours 30 minutes. When turkey is done, place on warm platter and cover with aluminum foil to keep warm. Let stand about 15 minutes for easiest carving. Garnish with whole chilies and additional sage leaves if desired.

7 While turkey is standing, skim fat from drippings. Pour just the drippings into 1-quart saucepan; heat to boiling. Serve with turkey. Cover and refrigerate any remaining turkey and stuffing separately.

1 Serving: Calories 310 (Calories from Fat 135); Fat 15g (Saturated 5g); Cholesterol 140mg; Sodium 140mg; Carbohydrate 0g (Dietary Fiber 0g); Protein 44g. **Diet Exchanges:** 6 Lean Meat.

Betty's Simple Substitution

For more great stuffing choices, try Wild Rice–Pecan Stuffing, page 54, or Vegetable-Herb Stuffing, page 55. Either would taste great with this Southwest-seasoned turkey.

High-Heat Roast Turkey

Prep: 10 min   **Roast:** 3 hr 15 min   **Stand:** 15 min   **25 servings**

20-pound turkey, thawed if frozen

1 teaspoon salt

1/2 teaspoon pepper

1 Move oven rack to lowest position. Heat oven to 450°. Prepare turkey for roasting as directed on page 15.

2 Fold wings across back of turkey so tips are touching. Rub both cavities lightly with salt and pepper.

3 Place turkey, breast side up, on rack in shallow roasting pan. Insert oven-proof meat thermometer so tip is in thickest part of inside thigh muscle and does not touch bone. (Do not add water or cover turkey.) Place turkey in oven with legs to the back of the oven to place them in hottest part of oven, if possible.

4 Roast uncovered 2 hours 45 minutes to 3 hours 15 minutes, watching carefully. After roasting about 1 hour 30 minutes, wearing oven mitts that cover hands and wrists, place a tent of aluminum foil loosely over turkey when it begins to turn golden.

5 Turkey is done when thermometer reads 180° and juice of turkey is no longer pink when you cut into center of thigh. The drumstick should move easily when lifted or twisted. If a meat thermometer is not used, begin testing for doneness after about 2 hours 15 minutes. When turkey is done, place on warm platter and cover with aluminum foil to keep warm. Let stand about 15 minutes for easiest carving.

1 Serving: Calories 275 (Calories from Fat 115); Fat 13g (Saturated 4g); Cholesterol 15mg; Sodium 190mg; Carbohydrate 0g (Dietary Fiber 0g); Protein 40g. **Diet Exchanges:** 5 Lean Meat.

Betty's Helpful Tip

Be sure to wear long oven mitts and take care when roasting at this higher temperature. Spattering in your oven may occur so it's best to start with a clean oven. You may need to clean it again after roasting—but save that chore for the next day!

All About
High-Heat Roasting

Unbelievable! You'll be pleasantly surprised to find that you can roast at a high temperature for a short amount of time and still achieve a turkey that's just as moist, tender and flavorful as one cooked by traditional lower-heat roasting.

High-heat roasting is a great time-saver, and best of all, you don't need any new or special equipment. This method produces a very moist bird and can save you a great deal of time, especially if you're cooking Thanksgiving dinner for a crowd. A 20-pound bird takes only 2 hours 45 minutes, compared to 4 hours 30 minutes when roasted at 325°. And because the bird is cooked at such a high temperature, it gives you an abundance of drippings to cook your gravy, and more of the fat drains off the turkey. See Roasting Timetable (page 16) if you would like to high-heat roast a turkey of another weight.

- Clean your oven beforehand, if needed, to keep it from smoking while cooking at high temperature.
- Wear long oven mitts and be watchful of spattering when checking on turkey.
- Place turkey in oven with legs to the back of the oven if possible. Since the legs take longer to cook than the breast, this places them in hottest part of oven.
- Never stuff a turkey that will be high-heat roasted. The stuffing won't cook through in the time that the turkey cooks.
- Some recipes for high-heat roasting suggest removing the breastbone before cooking, but that's not necessary. You can leave it in and get the same great results.

Grilled Lemon-Herb Turkey

Prep: 15 min   **Grill:** 3 hr 30 min   **Stand:** 15 min   **15 to 18 servings**

10- to 12-pound turkey, thawed if frozen

Salt and pepper, if desired

1 large onion, cut into eighths

2 small lemons, cut into fourths

Vegetable oil

2 tablespoons butter or margarine, softened

1/2 teaspoon ground thyme

1 If using charcoal grill, place drip pan directly under grilling area, and arrange coals around edge of firebox. Heat coals or gas grill for indirect heat.

2 Prepare turkey for roasting as directed on page 15.

3 Fasten neck skin to back of turkey with skewer. Fold wings across back of turkey so tips are touching. Rub cavity of turkey with salt and pepper; place onion and lemons in cavity. Brush oil over turkey. Insert barbecue meat thermometer so tip is in the thickest part of inside thigh muscle and does not touch bone.

4 Mix butter and thyme; brush over turkey. Cover and grill turkey, breast side up, over drip pan or over unheated side of gas grill and 5 to 6 inches from medium heat 2 hours 30 minutes to 3 hours 30 minutes. If using charcoal grill, add about 15 briquettes every hour.

5 Turkey is done when thermometer reads 180° and juice of turkey is no longer pink when you cut into center of thigh. The drumstick should move easily when lifted or twisted. If a meat thermometer is not used, begin testing for doneness after about 2 hours. When turkey is done, place on warm platter and cover with aluminum foil to keep warm. Let stand about 15 minutes for easiest carving.

1 Serving: Calories 290 (Calories from Fat 135); Fat 15g (Saturated 5g); Cholesterol 115mg; Sodium 100mg; Carbohydrate 0g (Dietary Fiber 0g); Protein 39g. **Diet Exchanges:** 5 Lean Meat.

All About Grilling

Grilling produces a delicious bird with crisp golden skin and frees up your oven for your other cooking and baking needs.

- Select a smaller 6- to 12-pound bird for grilling.
- Marinate for extra flavor. Place turkey in a glass container and add about 1/2 cup any-flavor marinade per pound of turkey. Marinate in the refrigerator from 15 minutes or up to 24 hours.
- Use indirect heat. For a gas grill: place turkey over a drip pan on the unlit portion of grill. For a charcoal grill: arrange coals around the edge of the firebox, and place a drip pan in the center. Keep cover closed.
- Allow about 12 to 15 minutes per pound for whole turkeys, but be sure to also check the manufacturer's recommendations for your grill.
- Do not stuff a turkey that will be grilled. The stuffing won't cook through in the time that the turkey cooks.

Betty's Helpful Tip

The meat of a whole turkey grilled as in this recipe will appear slightly pink when done but the juices will be clear. To be sure that your turkey is fully cooked, use a barbecue meat thermometer and grill until the internal temperature reaches 180°.

All About
Deep-Frying

Cooks down South have long enjoyed the tender, moist meat that deep-fried turkey yields. Growing in popularity because it produces crispy skin and moist meat—without being greasy—in a shorter time than any other cooking method, deep-frying has convinced cooks across America that this is the trendy way to go! Deep-frying takes some equipment and a little know-how: a **turkey deep-fat frying kit** (includes a 40- to 60-quart **pot, basket** and **propane gas tank attachment**) can be purchased at outdoor equipment and specialty kitchen stores. You will also need to buy or rent the propane tank.

Plan to use about 5 gallons of oil for a 10- to 12-pound turkey. You can choose to leave the turkey plain, or you can inject it with marinade or apply a seasoning rub. If you choose to use a marinade, you'll need a large syringe. Plan on approximately 1 cup marinade for a 10- to 12 pound turkey. Inject 2/3 cup into the breast and 1/3 cup into the thighs and drumsticks. Do *not* stuff a turkey that will be deep-fried because the stuffing will not cook through.

Frying oil can be reused. Cool oil completely, and strain through a fine sieve, cheesecloth or paper towels. Store the oil in a cool, dark area or in the refrigerator. When you're ready to use the oil again, add a small amount of fresh oil. If the oil develops an odor or off flavor, drop several slices of raw potato into the oil to absorb the odor. Remove the potato before frying the turkey. You can reuse the oil four or five times.

- Follow the use-and-care directions for your deep-fryer when deep-frying turkey, and review all safety tips.

- Have a fire extinguisher nearby for added safety.

- Place the fryer on a level dirt or grassy area away from the house or garage. Never fry a turkey indoors, including in a garage or any other structure attached to a building. If only concrete is available, place a large sheet of cardboard over area to prevent oil stains.

- Use an oil with a high smoke point, such as peanut oil. Soybean, canola or safflower oil can also be used.

- Before frying, a handy way to determine the correct amount of oil to use is to place the turkey in the basket and place in the pot. Add water until it reaches 1 to 2 inches above the turkey. Remove the turkey and note the water level, using a ruler to measure the distance from the top of the pot to the surface of the water. Pour out the water and dry the pot and turkey thoroughly. Be sure to measure before marinating turkey.

- Make sure turkey and any utensils used are completely dry before lowering into oil. Water added to oil can cause excessive bubbling.

- Wear old shoes that you can slip out of easily and long pants just in case you do spill some oil.

- Long sleeves and oven mitts will protect you from steam and oil spattering.

- Allow the oil to cool completely before disposing of or storing.

- Never place fryer on a wooden deck or other structure that could catch fire.

- Never leave the hot oil unattended, and do not allow children or pets near the cooking area.

- Do not fry a stuffed turkey.

Cajun Deep-Fried Turkey

Prep: 1 hr 15 min   Marinate: 8 hr   Cook: 42 min   Stand: 20 min   **15 to 18 servings**

Cajun Spice Rub (next page)

Cajun Marinade (next page), if desired

10- to 12-pound turkey, thawed if frozen

1 poultry or meat injector

1 turkey deep-fryer, consisting of 40- to 60-quart pot with basket, burner and propane tank

5 gallons peanut, canola or safflower oil

1 Read All About Deep-Frying (page 27).

2 Make Cajun Spice Rub and Cajun Marinade.

3 Prepare turkey for roasting as directed on page 15, taking extra care to dry inside both cavities, because water added to hot oil can cause excessive bubbling. To allow for good oil circulation through the cavity, do not tie the legs together. Cut off wing tips and tail because they can get caught in the fryer basket. Place turkey in large pan.

4 Rub inside and outside of turkey with spice rub. Inject marinade into turkey, following the directions that came with injector. Cover turkey in pan with plastic wrap and place in refrigerator at least 8 hours but no longer than 24 hours.

5 Place the outdoor gas burner on a level dirt or grassy area or on concrete covered with cardboard. Add oil to cooking pot only to fill line. Clip deep-fry thermometer to edge of pot. At medium-high setting, heat oil to 375°. (This can take 20 to 40 minutes depending on outside temperature, wind and weather conditions.) Place turkey, neck end down, on basket or rack. When deep-fry thermometer reaches 375°, very slowly lower turkey into hot oil, wearing long oven mitts on both hands. (Level of oil will rise due to frothing caused by moisture from the turkey but will stabilize in about 1 minute.)

6 Immediately check oil temperature and increase flame so oil temperature is maintained at 350°. (If temperature drops to 340° or below, oil will begin to seep into turkey.)

7 Fry turkey about 3 to 4 minutes per pound, or about 35 to 42 minutes for a 10- to 12-pound turkey. Stay with the fryer at all times because the heat may need to be regulated throughout frying.

8 At the minimum frying time, carefully remove turkey to check for doneness. A meat thermometer inserted into thickest part of thigh should read 180°. If necessary, return turkey to oil and continue cooking. When turkey is done, let it drain a few minutes.

9 Remove turkey from basket or rack and place on a serving platter. Cover with aluminum foil and let stand 15 minutes for easiest carving.

---

1 Serving: Calories 300 (Calories from Fat 90); Fat 14g (Saturated 4g); Cholesterol 120mg; Sodium 260mg; Carbohydrate 0g (Dietary Fiber 0g); Protein 42g. **Diet Exchanges:** 6 Lean Meat.

Betty's Helpful Tip

For best results when deep-frying, use cooking oils that can withstand high temperatures. Peanut, canola and safflower oils are at the top of the list! To learn more about deep-frying turkeys, visit the National Turkey Federation Web site at www.turkeyfed.org.

Cajun Spice Rub

2 tablespoons black pepper

1 tablespoon ground chipotle chilies or crushed red pepper

1 tablespoon white pepper

1 tablespoon ground cumin

1 tablespoon ground nutmeg

1 tablespoon salt

Mix all ingredients.

Cajun Marinade

1/2 cup vegetable oil

1/2 cup red wine vinegar

2 teaspoons sugar

2 teaspoons chili powder

1 teaspoon garlic powder

1 teaspoon salt

1/2 teaspoon ground pepper

Mix all ingredients in shallow glass or plastic dish until salt is dissolved.

Smoked Turkey

Prep: 40 min   **Cook:** 6 hr   **Stand:** 15 min   **12 servings**

Hickory or other hardwood (such as pecan or maple) or fruitwood (such as apple or cherry) chips or chunks

1 water smoker

1 bag (20 pounds) charcoal briquettes

Charcoal lighter fluid

10- to 12-pound turkey, thawed if frozen

2 tablespoons vegetable oil

1/2 teaspoon seasoned salt

About 2 to 3 quarts hot water

1 Read All About Water-Smoking (next page).

2 Cover wood chips with water; soak 30 minutes. Place the smoker in an area shielded from winds to maintain a consistent cooking temperature. To start fire, open vents of water-smoker. Fill vented pan with 10 pounds of charcoal briquettes. Pour 1/2 to 1 cup lighter fluid over the briquettes and let soak a few minutes. Light and wait until coals are hot and ashy-gray, about 30 minutes.

3 Prepare turkey for roasting as directed on page 15.

4 Fasten neck skin to back of turkey with skewer. Fold wings across back of turkey so tips are touching. Rub oil over turkey. Sprinkle seasoned salt inside cavities and on outside of turkey. Insert ovenproof meat thermometer so tip is in thickest part of inside thigh muscle and does not touch bone. Do *not* stuff turkey.

5 Wearing long oven mitts, set the water pan in place. Carefully pour hot water into the pan until it is three-fourths full. Lightly brush food rack with vegetable oil; place in smoker above water pan. Place lid on smoker; wait for the internal temperature to reach 220° to 250°. (Some smokers have built-in temperature indicators; if yours does not, use an oven thermometer to determine temperature.) When heated, quickly place turkey on top rack.

6 Cover and smoke turkey 5 to 6 hours. Place 2 handfuls of damp wood chips over hot coals through the side door, then add handfuls every couple of hours during the cooking process. Add charcoal as needed to maintain temperature, about every 1 to 1 1/2 hours. After about 3 hours, refill the water pan if necessary.

7 Turkey is done when thermometer reads 180° and juice of turkey is no longer pink when you cut into center of thigh. The drumstick should move easily when lifted or twisted. If a meat thermometer is not used, begin testing for doneness after about 4 1/2 hours. When turkey is done, place on warm platter and cover with aluminum foil to keep warm. Let stand about 15 minutes for easiest carving.

1 Serving: Calories 340 (Calories from Fat 155); Fat 17g (Saturated 5g); Cholesterol 130mg; Sodium 170mg; Carbohydrate 0g (Dietary Fiber 0g); Protein 46g. **Diet Exchanges:** 6 Lean Meat.

Betty's Simple Substitution

For extra smoked flavor, you can add the liquid drained from the wood chips or some wine or apple juice, to flavor the hot water.

All About
Water-Smoking

Smoked turkey is very tender and juicy and has a unique deep-smoked flavor. The secret is the slow cooking, but you will also need some special equipment. You can purchase a **smoker** at an outdoor equipment or specialty kitchen store. You should also have an **oven thermometer** if your smoker doesn't have a built-in temperature indicator, an ovenproof meat thermometer and flavorful hardwood or fruitwood chips or chunks. You will also need a lot of patience, because roasting a 12- to 14-pound turkey can take 6 to 8 hours. If you choose this method, turn it into an all-day entertainment! Make sure you have lots of helpers around to take over checking and adding charcoal and wood to the smoker when you want to take a break.

- Estimate roughly 30 minutes per pound of cooking if smoker is running at 240°. A 12-pound turkey needs at least 6 hours and even more if the smoker is at a lower temperature.

- Always use a meat thermometer.

- Always wear long oven mitts made for outdoor cooking.

- Hardwood or fruitwood chips or chunks, such as hickory, pecan, maple, apple or cherry, produce aromatic smoke that gives your turkey great flavor. You can buy bags of wood chips at a hardware or specialty kitchen store.

- Heat and liquid are critical to maintaining the hot smoke that cooks the turkey. Avoid opening the cover or door as much as possible since this results in quick heat loss. Smoking takes place at low temperatures; maintaining the temperature is critical or cooking time must increase.

- Do not stuff a turkey that will be smoked.

- Don't use evergreen or other resinous wood in your smoker. Mesquite is not recommended for smoking because it imparts a very strong flavor.

Brined Whole Turkey

Soak: 8 hr   **Prep:** 15 min   **Roast:** 4 hr   **Stand:** 15 min   **14 servings**

12- to 14-pound turkey (not prebasted), thawed if frozen

2 gallons cold water

2 cups kosher salt or 1 cup table salt

1 medium onion, cut into fourths

1 medium carrot, coarsely chopped

1 medium stalk celery, coarsely chopped

1 teaspoon dried thyme leaves

3 tablespoons unsalted butter, melted

1 Read Turkey Brining Do's and Don'ts (next page).

2 Prepare turkey for roasting as directed on page 15, but do not rub cavities with salt.

3 Mix cold water and salt in a large clean bucket or stockpot (noncorrosive); stir until salt is dissolved. Add turkey. Cover and refrigerate 8 to 12 hours.

4 Heat oven to 325°. Remove turkey from brine; discard brine. Thoroughly rinse turkey under cool running water, gently rubbing outside and inside of turkey to release salt. Pat skin and both interior cavities dry with paper towels.

5 Fasten neck skin to back of turkey with skewer. Fold wings across back of turkey so tips are touching. Toss onion, carrot, celery and thyme with 1 tablespoon of the melted butter; place in turkey cavity.

6 Place turkey, breast side down, on rack in large shallow roasting pan. Brush entire back side of turkey with 1 tablespoon melted butter. Turn turkey over. Brush entire breast side of turkey with remaining 1 table-spoon melted butter. Insert ovenproof meat thermometer so tip is in thickest part of inside thigh muscle and does not touch bone. (Do not add water or cover turkey.)

7 Roast uncovered 3 hours 30 minutes to 4 hours, brushing twice with pan drippings during last 30 minutes of roasting.

8 Turkey is done when thermometer reads 180° and juice of turkey is no longer pink when you cut into center of thigh. The drumstick should move easily when lifted or twisted. If a meat thermometer is not used, begin testing for doneness after about 3 hours. When turkey is done, place on warm platter and cover with aluminum foil to keep warm. Let stand about 15 minutes for easiest carving.

1 Serving: Calories 325 (Calories from Fat 135); Fat 15g (Saturated 5g); Cholesterol 145mg; Sodium 620mg; Carbohydrate 0g (Dietary Fiber 0g); Protein 47g. **Diet Exchanges:** 7 Lean Meat.

Betty's Do-Ahead

Turkey can be brined a day ahead. Rinse well, cover and refrigerate until time to roast.

All About
Brining

For exceptionally moist and tender meat, brining is the way to go! Immersing your turkey in a saltwater bath (the brine) overnight draws water into the cells of the turkey so it stays juicy and moist when cooked. For this method, you'll need a large clean plastic bucket or noncorrosive stockpot (not aluminum), enough refrigerator space and time, but it's a great do-ahead.

- Use a large clean plastic bucket or a stainless steel stockpot or other noncorrosive container that can fit the turkey and enough brine to keep turkey submerged.

- Keep turkey refrigerated while it is brining. You may have to clear a space in your refrigerator to accommodate the bucket or stockpot.

- Check the temperature frequently as the turkey is roasting since a brined turkey may cook slightly faster than an unbrined one.

- Do not soak turkey in brine for more than 12 hours because it will absorb too much salt.

- Do not stuff a brined turkey with stuffing.

- Some brines create turkey drippings and juices that are too salty to make good gravy while others make delicious gravy, so follow the recipe directions carefully. No-Drippings Gravy (page 49) is a great choice if the drippings are too salty.

Best Brined Turkey Breast

Soak: 12 hr   **Prep:** 10 min   **Roast:** 2 hr 30 min   8 to 10 servings

9 cups hot water

3/4 cup salt

1/2 cup sugar

4- to 6-pound bone-in whole turkey breast, thawed if frozen

1 small onion, sliced

2 fresh rosemary sprigs

4 fresh thyme sprigs

3 dried bay leaves

6 tablespoons butter or margarine, melted

1/4 cup dry white wine or chicken broth

1 Mix hot water, salt and sugar in 6-quart container or stockpot; stir until salt and sugar are dissolved. Add turkey. Cover and refrigerate at least 12 hours but no longer than 24 hours.

2 Heat oven to 325°. Remove turkey from brine; discard brine. Thoroughly rinse turkey under cool running water, gently rubbing to release salt. Pat dry with paper towels.

3 Place turkey on rack in shallow roasting pan. Place onion, rosemary, thyme and bay leaves on turkey. Insert ovenproof meat thermometer so tip is in thickest part of turkey and does not touch bone.

4 Mix butter and wine. Soak 16-inch square of cheesecloth in butter mixture until completely saturated; cover turkey, onion and herbs completely with cheesecloth.

5 Roast 2 to 2 1/2 hours. After 1 1/2 hours, remove cheesecloth. Remove onion and herbs from turkey, but leave in pan. Turn turkey over so back side is up. Roast 30 to 60 minutes longer or until thermometer reads 170° and juice of turkey is no longer pink when you cut into the center. If a meat thermometer is not used, begin testing for doneness after about 2 hours.

1 Serving: Calories 355 (Calories from Fat 180); Fat 20g (Saturated 8g); Cholesterol 140mg; Sodium 1030mg; Carbohydrate 1g (Dietary Fiber 0g); Protein 43g. **Diet Exchanges:** 6 Lean Meat.

Betty's Special Touch

This turkey makes delicious herb-scented gravy (strain the onion and herbs from the drippings). Follow the Classic Pan Gravy recipe on page 48.

Butter- and Wine-Basted Turkey Breast

Prep: 15 min   **Roast:** 2 hr 30 min   **Stand:** 15 min   **8 to 10 servings**

(see photo insert)

4 1/2- to 5-pound bone-in whole turkey breast, thawed if frozen

1/2 cup butter or margarine, melted

1/4 cup dry white wine or apple juice

2 tablespoons chopped fresh or 1 1/2 teaspoons dried thyme leaves

1 teaspoon salt

1 teaspoon paprika

2 cloves garlic, finely chopped

2 teaspoons cornstarch

2 tablespoons cold water

1 Heat oven to 325°. Place turkey, skin side up, on rack in shallow roasting pan. Insert ovenproof meat thermometer so tip is in thickest part of turkey and does not touch bone.

2 Roast 2 to 2 1/2 hours. While turkey is roasting, mix butter, wine, thyme, salt, paprika and garlic. After 1 hour, brush turkey with half of the butter mixture. Roast uncovered 30 minutes more; brush with remaining butter mixture. Roast uncovered about 1 hour longer or until thermometer reads 170° and juice of turkey is no longer pink when you cut into the center. If a meat thermometer is not used, begin testing for doneness after about 2 hours. When turkey is done, place on warm platter and cover with aluminum foil to keep warm. Let stand about 15 minutes for easiest carving.

3 While turkey is standing, pour pan drippings into measuring cup; skim fat from drippings. Add enough water to drippings to measure 2 cups. Heat drippings to boiling in 1-quart saucepan. Mix cornstarch and cold water; stir into drippings. Boil and stir 1 minute. Serve gravy with turkey.

1 Serving: Calories 420 (Calories from Fat 225); Fat 25g (Saturated 11g); Cholesterol 165mg; Sodium 480mg; Carbohydrate 1g (Dietary Fiber 0g); Protein 48g. **Diet Exchanges:** 7 Lean Meat, 1 Fat.

Betty's Special Touch

Garnish with small whole apples and fresh herbs such as thyme or sage.

Slow Cooker Turkey Breast Stuffed with Wild Rice and Cranberries

Prep: 25 min   **Cook:** 9 hr

10 servings

4 cups cooked wild rice

3/4 cup finely chopped onion

1/2 cup dried cranberries

1/3 cup slivered almonds

2 medium peeled or unpeeled cooking apples, coarsely chopped (2 cups)

4- to 5-pound boneless whole turkey breast, thawed if frozen

1 Mix all ingredients except turkey. Cut turkey into slices at 1-inch intervals about three-fourths of the way through, forming deep pockets.

2 Place turkey in 3 1/2- to 6-quart slow cooker. Stuff pockets with wild rice mixture. Place remaining rice mixture around edge of cooker.

3 Cover and cook on low heat setting 8 to 9 hours or until turkey is no longer pink in center.

1 **Serving:** Calories 415 (Calories from Fat 125); Fat 14g (Saturated 3g); Cholesterol 115mg; Sodium 100mg; Carbohydrate 26g (Dietary Fiber 4g); Protein 47g. **Diet Exchanges:** 2 Starch, 6 Very Lean Meat, 1 Fat.

Betty's Do-Ahead

You'll be ready to stuff the turkey breast if you cook the wild rice ahead of time. Start with 1 1/3 cups uncooked wild rice, and add 3 cups water. Heat to boiling, reduce heat and simmer over low heat 40 to 50 minutes or until water is absorbed. The cooked wild rice and other stuffing ingredients also can be combined ahead and refrigerated, but for food safety reasons, do not stuff the turkey breast until ready to cook.

Easy Turkey and Vegetables Dinner

Prep: 20 min   **Roast:** 2 hr 30 min   **Stand:** 15 min   **10 to 12 servings**

4 1/2- to 5-pound bone-in whole turkey breast, thawed if frozen

10 medium potatoes

10 medium carrots, cut diagonally into 2-inch pieces

1/2 cup butter or margarine, melted

1/4 cup dry white wine or apple juice

2 tablespoons chopped fresh or 1 1/2 teaspoons dried rosemary leaves

1 teaspoon salt

1 teaspoon paprika

2 cloves garlic, finely chopped

2 teaspoons cornstarch

2 tablespoons cold water

Chopped fresh parsley, if desired

1 Heat oven to 325°. Place turkey breast, skin side up, on rack in shallow roasting pan. Insert ovenproof meat thermometer so tip is in thickest part of turkey and does not touch bone. Cut potatoes crosswise into 1/4-inch slices about three-fourths of the way through. Place potatoes and carrots on rack around turkey.

2 Mix butter, wine, rosemary, salt, paprika and garlic. Brush vegetables with about one-fourth of the butter mixture.

3 Roast uncovered 2 to 2 1/2 hours. After 1 hour, brush turkey and vegetables with half of the remaining butter mixture. Roast 30 minutes more; then brush with remaining butter mixture. Roast about 1 hour longer or until vegetables are tender, thermometer reads 170° and juice of turkey is no longer pink when you cut into the center. If a meat thermometer is not used, begin testing for doneness after about 2 hours. When turkey is done, place turkey and vegetables on warm platter and cover with aluminum foil to keep warm. Let turkey stand about 15 minutes for easiest carving.

4 While turkey is standing, pour pan drippings into measuring cup; skim fat from drippings. Add enough water to drippings to measure 2 cups. Heat drippings to boiling in 1-quart saucepan. Mix cornstarch and cold water; stir into drippings. Boil and stir 1 minute. Serve gravy with turkey. Sprinkle parsley over carrots.

---

1 Serving: Calories 470 (Calories from Fat 180); Fat 20g (Saturated 9g); Cholesterol 130mg; Sodium 410mg; Carbohydrate 31g (Dietary Fiber 4g); Protein 41g. **Diet Exchanges:** 1 1/2 Starch, 5 Lean Meat, 1 Vegetable, 1 Fat.

Betty's Helpful Tip

While carving, keep the turkey from moving by holding it in place with a meat fork. Carve on a stable cutting surface, such as a plastic cutting board or platter.

Homemade Turkey Soup

Prep: 30 min   **Cook:** 2 hr 25 min   **9 servings**

Bones and trimmings from cooked 9- to 15-pound turkey

3 quarts (12 cups) water

1 teaspoon salt

1/2 teaspoon pepper

1/4 teaspoon poultry seasoning or dried sage leaves

1 dried bay leaf

1/2 cup uncooked barley

3 medium carrots, sliced (1 1/2 cups)

1 large onion, chopped (1 cup)

2 medium stalks celery, sliced (1 cup)

2 tablespoons chopped fresh parsley

1 Break up turkey to fit 6-quart Dutch oven. Add water, salt, pepper, poultry seasoning and bay leaf. Heat to boiling over high heat; reduce heat to low. Cover and simmer 1 hour 30 minutes.

2 Skim off any residue that rises to the surface. Remove bones, meat and bay leaf from broth; cool. When cool enough to handle, remove meat from bones and cut into bite-size pieces; set aside. Discard bones and bay leaf.

3 Skim fat from broth; discard. Add turkey meat to broth; stir in barley. Heat to boiling; reduce heat to low. Cover and simmer 30 minutes, stirring occasionally.

4 Stir in carrots, onion and celery. Simmer 20 to 25 minutes longer or until vegetables and barley are tender. Stir in parsley.

1 Serving: Calories 165 (Calories from Fat 35); Fat 4g (Saturated 1g); Cholesterol 35mg; Sodium 340mg; Carbohydrate 15g (Dietary Fiber 3g); Protein 17g. **Diet Exchanges:** 1 Starch, 2 Very Lean Meat.

Homemade Turkey Vegetable Soup: Add up to 3 cups raw or cooked vegetables such as whole kernel corn, green peas, diced potatoes, sliced zucchini, sliced mushrooms or any combination along with the carrots, onion and celery.

Betty's Simple Substitution

If the turkey cut from the bones does not measure 3 cups, add additional cut-up cooked turkey. 3/4 cup uncooked cracked bulgur, 1/2 cup uncooked regular long-grain white rice or 1 1/2 cups uncooked egg noodles can be substituted for the barley. Add the bulgur, rice or noodles to the broth with the vegetables after heating the broth and turkey meat to boiling. Continue as directed.

Turkey Tetrazzini

Prep: 15 min   **Cook:** 10 min   **Bake:** 30 min   **5 servings**

1 package (7 ounces)
spaghetti, broken into
thirds

1/4 cup butter or
margarine

1/4 cup all-purpose flour

1/2 teaspoon salt

1/4 teaspoon pepper

3/4 cup chicken or
turkey broth

1 1/4 cups milk

2 cups cubed cooked
turkey

1 can (4 ounces) sliced
mushrooms, drained

1/2 cup grated Parmesan
cheese

1 Heat oven to 350°. Cook spaghetti as directed on package.

2 While spaghetti is cooking, melt butter in 3-quart saucepan over medium heat. Stir in flour, salt and pepper. Cook, stirring constantly, until mixture is bubbly; remove from heat. Stir in broth and milk. Heat to boiling, stirring constantly. Boil and stir 1 minute. Stir in turkey and mushrooms.

3 Drain spaghetti; place in ungreased 2-quart casserole. Stir in turkey mixture. Sprinkle with cheese. Bake uncovered about 30 minutes or until hot and bubbly.

1 Serving: Calories 435 (Calories from Fat 160); Fat 18g (Saturated 10g); Cholesterol 85mg; Sodium 810mg; Carbohydrate 41g (Dietary Fiber 2g); Protein 29g. **Diet Exchanges:** 3 Starch, 3 Medium-Fat Meat.

Betty's Do-Ahead

You can prepare and bake this casserole ahead of time and freeze it, tightly wrapped, for up to 2 months. When ready to serve, heat oven to 350° and bake frozen casserole, covered, about 40 minutes or until hot and bubbly.

Turkey and Stuffing Casserole

Prep: 15 min   **Bake:** 35 min   **6 servings**

1 can (10 3/4 ounces) condensed cream of chicken or celery soup

1/2 cup milk

1 cup frozen green peas

1/2 cup dried cranberries

4 medium green onions, sliced (1/4 cup)

2 cups cut-up cooked turkey

1 1/2 cups cooked corn bread stuffing or other leftover stuffing

1 cup Original Bisquick®

1/4 cup milk

2 eggs

1 Heat oven to 400°. Spray 3-quart casserole with cooking spray. Heat soup and 1/2 cup milk to boiling in 3-quart saucepan, stirring frequently. Stir in peas, cranberries and onions. Heat to boiling, stirring frequently; remove from heat. Stir in turkey and stuffing. Spoon into casserole.

2 Stir remaining ingredients until blended. Pour over stuffing mixture.

3 Bake uncovered 30 to 35 minutes or until knife inserted in center comes out clean.

1 **Serving:** Calories 395 (Calories from Fat 145); Fat 16g (Saturated 4g); Cholesterol 115mg; Sodium 1010mg; Carbohydrate 41g (Dietary Fiber 3g); Protein 22g. **Diet Exchanges:** 3 Starch, 2 Lean Meat, 1 Fat.

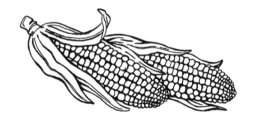

Betty's Simple Substitution

Use your leftover turkey and stuffing to create this cozy casserole. Serve with a side of cranberry-orange relish or cranberry sauce. No dried cranberries on hand? You can leave them out of the recipe or use dried cherries or raisins instead.

Stuffed Turkey, Ham and Swiss Rolls

Prep: 15 min

1 1/2 cups leftover cooked stuffing (any variety)

1 cup chopped cooked turkey

6 slices (1 ounce each) cooked ham

1/4 cup chicken broth

3 slices (3/4 ounce each) Swiss cheese, cut in half

Chopped fresh parsley, if desired

1 Mix stuffing and turkey. Place about 1/3 cup stuffing mixture on center of each ham slice. Roll ham around mixture; place in large skillet.

2 Add broth to skillet. Cover and cook over medium heat 7 to 10 minutes or until thoroughly heated. Place 1 piece of cheese over each roll during last 30 to 60 seconds of cooking time. Sprinkle with parsley.

1 Roll: Calories 215 (Calories from Fat 100); Fat 11g (Saturated 4g); Cholesterol 45mg; Sodium 780mg; Carbohydrate 11g (Dietary Fiber 0g); Protein 18g. **Diet Exchanges:** 1 Starch, 2 Lean Meat, 1 Fat.

Betty's Simple Substitution

If you have leftover turkey gravy, mix a little of it with the broth before heating the broth in step 2.

Cranberry–Turkey Salad

Prep: 20 min

4 servings

1 cup Classic Cranberry Sauce (page 59) or other homemade cranberry sauce

1/2 cup orange juice

1 bag (10 ounces) mixed salad greens (about 6 cups)

2 cups cubed cooked turkey

2 oranges, peeled and cut into segments

1 Heat Classic Cranberry Sauce and orange juice in 1-quart saucepan over low heat, stirring occasionally, just until warmed; remove from heat.

2 Arrange salad greens, turkey and orange segments on 4 individual serving plates. Drizzle cranberry dressing over salads.

1 Serving: Calories 305 (Calories from Fat 45); Fat 5g (Saturated 1g); Cholesterol 60mg; Sodium 95mg; Carbohydrate 43g (Dietary Fiber 4g); Protein 22g. **Diet Exchanges:** 2 Lean Meat, 3 Vegetable, 2 Fruit.

Betty's Special Touch

Use your leftover turkey and cranberry sauce to create this tasty and colorful salad. Garnish with sliced almonds for extra crunch.

Turkey Club Wraps

Prep: 15 min

2 slices bacon, cut in half

1/4 cup mayonnaise or salad dressing

1/4 cup medium salsa

4 flour tortillas (10 inches in diameter), heated

4 large leaves romaine lettuce

2 cups chopped cooked turkey

1 Cook bacon in 12-inch nonstick skillet over medium heat, turning occasionally, until crisp. Drain on paper towels.

2 While bacon is cooking, mix mayonnaise and salsa.

3 Top each warm tortilla with lettuce, turkey, mayonnaise mixture and bacon. Fold both sides of each tortilla toward center, overlapping slightly; secure each with 2 toothpicks. Cut each in half.

1 Wrap: Calories 460 (Calories from Fat 200); Fat 22g (Saturated 5g); Cholesterol 70mg; Sodium 580mg; Carbohydrate 39g (Dietary Fiber 3g); Protein 27g. **Diet Exchanges:** 2 1/2 Starch, 3 Lean Meat, 2 Fat.

Betty's Special Touch

For variety, try herb- or tomato-flavored tortillas. Add sliced cheese, tomatoes, bell peppers or other toppings to make your sandwiches sensational!

Gravy, Stuffing *and* Sauces

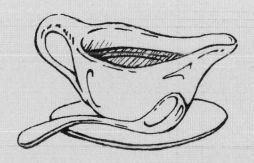

Great Gravy

Who doesn't love gravy? One of the most frequently asked cooking questions is "How do I make good gravy?" Though it's simple once you've made it a few times, making gravy the first time can be a bit tricky. The first step is to transfer the turkey to a warm platter and keep it warm while you're making the gravy. Then, whisk up your smoothest and best-tasting gravy ever with these terrific tips!

Smooth Secrets

- Keep it lump-free by using a wire whisk when adding the flour to the drippings. Beat the drippings rapidly with the whisk while adding the flour, and there won't be any lumps.

- Measure ingredients accurately. (Too little fat can make the gravy lumpy; too much fat can make the gravy greasy.)

- Be sure the mixture cooks at a full boil for 1 minute to cook the flour or cornstarch so the gravy doesn't have a starchy flavor.

- If you don't have enough drippings, you can use water from cooking potatoes or sweet potatoes, wine or tomato or eight-vegetable juice.

- If you have plenty of pan drippings and like lots of gravy or are serving a crowd you can double or triple the recipe.

- If you don't have flour on hand, don't worry! You can use Bisquick; or substitute cornstarch for shiny, translucent gravy; or substitute Wondra® quick-mixing flour for quick-mixing gravy.

- For thinner gravy, decrease meat drippings and flour to 1 tablespoon each.

Making Gravy

Return drippings to the roasting pan, then stir in flour.

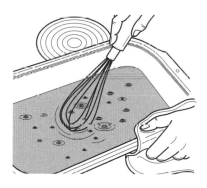

Stir in the turkey juices. Heat to boiling, stirring constantly. Cook over low heat, stirring constantly and scraping up brown bits, until mixture is smooth and bubbly.

Gravy Rx

What if my gravy is:	Quick Fixes
Greasy	Place a slice of fresh bread on top of the fat for a few seconds to absorb it; remove bread before it breaks into pieces.
Lumpy	Pour into food processor and process until smooth or press gravy through a strainer; return to saucepan and heat.
Too thin	Dissolve 1 tablespoon flour in 2 tablespoons water; stir into gravy with fork or wire whisk. Boil, stirring, 1 minute.
Too thick	Add additional milk or water.
Too pale in color	Stir in browning sauce, soy sauce or Worcestershire sauce (start with 1 teaspoon).
Too salty	Add a raw peeled potato, cut into eighths; cook and stir 5 to 10 minutes, then remove potato pieces. Or stir in 1/2 teaspoon sugar; taste and add a little more sugar, a teaspoon at a time, until less salty to taste. Adding a teaspoon of white vinegar with the sugar helps balance flavors.

Classic Pan Gravy

Prep: 10 min   **Cook:** 8 min

About 1 cup gravy

Drippings from roasted turkey

1 cup liquid (turkey juices, broth, water)

2 tablespoons all-purpose flour

Browning sauce, if desired

Salt and pepper to taste

1 After removing turkey from roasting pan, pour drippings (turkey juices and fat) into bowl or glass measuring cup, leaving brown bits in pan. Let drippings stand 5 minutes to allow fat to rise. Skim 2 tablespoons fat from top of drippings and return to pan; discard any remaining fat. Add enough broth or water to remaining drippings to measure 1 cup; reserve.

2 Stir flour into fat in pan. Cook over low heat, stirring constantly and scraping up brown bits, until mixture is smooth and bubbly; remove from heat.

3 Gradually stir in reserved 1 cup drippings. Heat to boiling, stirring constantly. Boil and stir 1 minute. Stir in a few drops of browning sauce if a darker color is desired. Stir in salt and pepper.

1/4 Cup: Calories 80 (Calories from Fat 65); Fat 7g (Saturated 2g); Cholesterol 5mg; Sodium 550mg; Carbohydrate 4g (Dietary Fiber 0g); Protein 1g. **Diet Exchanges:** 1 1/2 Fat.

Easy-Mixing Gravy: Substitute quick-mixing flour for the all-purpose flour.

Bisquick Mix Gravy: Substitute Bisquick for the all-purpose flour.

Thin Gravy: Decrease turkey drippings to 1 tablespoon and flour to 1 tablespoon.

Old-Fashioned Gravy: Substitute cooking water from potatoes or sweet potatoes for all or part of the liquid.

Vegetable Juice Gravy: Substitute tomato juice or eight-vegetable juice for part of the liquid.

Betty's Helpful Tip

White wine, dry sherry or Madeira wine add a wonderful flavor to gravy. Replace half of liquid with your choice of wine.

No-Drippings Gravy

Prep: 5 min **Cook:** 10 min

2 cups gravy

2 cups chicken or homemade turkey broth

2 teaspoons chicken bouillon granules

Dash of pepper

1/4 cup all-purpose flour

Browning sauce, if desired

1 Heat 1 1/2 cups of the broth, the bouillon granules and pepper in 1-quart heavy saucepan over medium heat, stirring constantly, until bouillon granules are dissolved.

2 Stir remaining 1/2 cup broth and the flour in small bowl, using wire whisk, until smooth. Gradually stir flour mixture into broth in saucepan. Heat to boiling. Cook, stirring constantly, until thickened and bubbly. Stir in a few drops of browning sauce if a darker color is desired.

1/4 Cup: Calories 25 (Calories from Fat 0); Fat 0g (Saturated 0g); Cholesterol 0mg; Sodium 520mg; Carbohydrate 4g (Dietary Fiber 0g); Protein 2g. **Diet Exchanges:** 1 Serving is free.

Creamy Gravy: Substitute 1 cup milk, half-and-half, whipping (heavy) cream or evaporated milk for 1 cup of the broth.

Betty's Helpful Tip

You asked for it! If you're grilling, deep-frying or smoking your turkey this year, you won't have turkey drippings—but you can still serve this luscious gravy.

Milk Gravy

Prep: 15 min   **Cook:** 7 min

2 1/2 cups gravy

1/4 cup drippings from roasted turkey

2 1/4 cups milk, heated

1/4 cup all-purpose flour

1/4 cup cold milk

Salt and pepper to taste

1 After removing turkey from roasting pan, leave drippings (turkey juices and fat) in roasting pan or add to 10-inch skillet. Stir heated milk into drippings.

2 Mix flour and cold milk in small bowl until smooth. Stir flour mixture into hot milk mixture. Cook over medium heat, stirring constantly and scraping up brown bits in pan, until boiling and thickened. Stir in salt and pepper.

1/4 Cup: Calories 40 (Calories from Fat 10); Fat 1g (Saturated 1g); Cholesterol 5mg; Sodium 110mg; Carbohydrate 5g (Dietary Fiber 0g); Protein 2g. **Diet Exchanges:** 1/2 Milk.

Betty's Helpful Tip

Make it your way! If you like thinner gravy, add 2 to 3 tablespoons more cold milk. If you prefer it thicker, add 1 tablespoon flour dissolved in 2 tablespoons cold water. Heat to boiling, stirring constantly.

Giblet Gravy

Prep: 15 min   **Cook:** 2 hr 5 min   **2 cups gravy**

Turkey giblets (from whole turkey, thawed if frozen)

2 medium stalks celery, sliced (1 cup)

1 medium onion, sliced

1 teaspoon salt

1/4 teaspoon pepper

Drippings from roasted turkey

About 1/4 cup chicken broth, if needed

1/4 cup all-purpose flour

Salt and pepper to taste

1 Place giblets (except liver) in 2-quart saucepan; add enough water to cover. Add celery, onion, salt and pepper. Heat to boiling; reduce heat to low. Cover and simmer 1 to 2 hours or until giblets are tender. Add liver during last 15 minutes of cooking.

2 Drain giblet mixture, reserving broth and giblets. Discard celery and onion.

3 After removing turkey from roasting pan, remove 1/2 cup drippings (turkey juices and fat); reserve. Pour remaining drippings into 2-cup measuring cup; add enough giblet broth and chicken broth to measure 2 cups; set aside.

4 Place reserved 1/2 cup drippings in roasting pan or 12-inch skillet. Stir in flour. Cook over low heat, stirring constantly and scraping up brown bits in pan, until smooth and browned. Gradually stir in 2 cups broth mixture. Cook, stirring constantly, until mixture boils and thickens. Remove meat from neck and finely chop with giblets and add to gravy if desired. Stir in salt and pepper.

1/4 Cup: Calories 90 (Calories from Fat 55); Fat 6g (Saturated 2g); Cholesterol 85mg; Sodium 300mg; Carbohydrate 3g (Dietary Fiber 0g); Protein 6g. **Diet Exchanges:** 1 Very Lean Meat, 1 Fat.

Betty's Do-Ahead

You can cook the giblet stock ahead of time. Follow directions above through step 2. If not using cooked giblets in gravy, discard. If using, cover and refrigerate the giblets and broth separately.

All About Giblets

Q. **What is that package of insides from the turkey, anyway? What do I do with it?**

A. The edible innards of birds, chicken and turkey, the **giblets**, are made up of the heart, gizzard, liver and neck. They are usually packaged in small paper bags and tucked inside the bird. Giblets make great gravy, or they can be cut up and mixed into a bread stuffing to make Giblet Stuffing (page 52).

Classic Bread Stuffing

Prep: 15 min   **Cook:** 5 min   **10 servings (1/2 cup each)**

3/4 cup butter or margarine

2 large stalks celery (with leaves), chopped (1 1/2 cups)

1 large onion, chopped (1 cup)

9 cups soft bread cubes (about 15 slices bread)

1 1/2 teaspoons chopped fresh or 1/2 teaspoon dried thyme leaves

1 teaspoon salt

1/2 teaspoon ground sage

1/4 teaspoon pepper

1 Melt butter in 4-quart Dutch oven over medium-high heat. Cook celery and onion in butter, stirring occasionally, until tender; remove from heat.

2 Toss celery mixture and remaining ingredients. Use to stuff one 10- to 12-pound turkey. See Turkey Talk (page 14) for specific directions.

1 Serving: Calories 215 (Calories from Fat 135); Fat 15g (Saturated 9g); Cholesterol 40mg; Sodium 510mg; Carbohydrate 18g (Dietary Fiber 1g); Protein 3g. **Diet Exchanges:** 1 Starch, 3 Fat.

Lighter Classic Bread Stuffing: For 6 grams of fat and 135 calories per serving, decrease butter to 1/4 cup. Heat butter and 1/2 cup chicken broth to boiling in Dutch oven over medium-high heat. Cook celery and onion in broth mixture. Continue as directed in step 2. 10 servings (1/2 cup each).

Apple-Raisin Stuffing: Increase salt to 1 1/2 teaspoons. Add 3 cups finely chopped apples and 3/4 cup raisins with the remaining ingredients. 15 servings (1/2 cup each).

Chestnut Stuffing: Add 1 to 1 1/2 cups roasted chestnuts, shelled and chopped, to stuffing. To roast chestnuts, cut X-shaped slit on one side of shell. Place on ungreased cookie sheet. Bake at 400° for 15 to 20 minutes, stirring occasionally. Cool slightly; remove shells. 12 servings (1/2 cup each).

Corn Bread Stuffing: Substitute corn bread cubes for the soft bread cubes. Use Southern Buttermilk Corn Bread (page 123) or purchase corn bread in the bakery section of the supermarket. 10 servings (1/2 cup each).

Giblet Stuffing: Simmer heart, gizzard and neck from turkey in water seasoned with salt and pepper 1 to 2 hours or until tender. Add liver during the last 15 minutes of cooking. Drain giblets. Remove meat from neck and finely chop with giblets; add with the remaining ingredients. 12 servings (1/2 cup each).

Mushroom Stuffing: Cook 2 cups sliced mushrooms (about 5 ounces) with the celery and onion. 10 servings (1/2 cup each).

Oyster Stuffing: Add 2 cans (8 ounces each) oysters, drained and chopped, or 2 cups shucked oysters, drained and chopped, with the remaining ingredients. 12 servings (1/2 cup each).

Sausage Stuffing: Omit salt. Cook 1 pound bulk pork sausage in 10-inch skillet over medium heat, stirring occasionally, until no longer pink; drain, reserving drippings. Substitute drippings for part of the butter. Add cooked sausage with the remaining ingredients. 12 servings (1/2 cup each).

Betty's Do-Ahead

Some cooks prefer to bake stuffing separately; place in a greased 3-quart casserole or rectangular baking dish, 13 × 9 × 2 inches, and bake covered at 325° for 30 minutes, then uncover and bake 15 minutes longer. To add turkey flavor, baste with juices from the turkey roasting pan.

The Right Stuff

Classic stuffing is usually made with white bread, but for variety you can try just about any kind: whole grain, sourdough, rye, French, Italian, herb or corn bread. Stale bread actually is best because it's easier to cut, doesn't get soft and mushy during baking, and will have a more fluffy texture than stuffing made with fresh. Some people prefer rice stuffing and others love stuffing made with meat or vegetables. The fastest way to homemade stuffing, when you're tight on time, is to use packaged croutons or stuffing mix. Prepare the stuffing just before you are ready to stuff the turkey, allowing about 3/4 cup stuffing per pound of poultry.

Start with Stuffing

- Pack stuffing in turkey *loosely* into the neck and body cavities of the turkey. (Stuffing expands while it bakes.)

- Don't prestuff a turkey and then put it in the refrigerator or freezer for later roasting; always stuff it just before cooking. (This prevents bacteria from contaminating stuffing.)

- Cook stuffing until center of stuffing reaches 165° to avoid any food safety issues.

- Place any extra stuffing in a covered casserole dish alongside the poultry. Uncover during the last 30 to 45 minutes of baking so the top can get nicely crisp, crunchy and golden brown.

- If you are grilling, deep-frying, smoking or high-heat roasting your turkey, bake the stuffing separately. Place in a greased 3-quart casserole or rectangular baking dish, 13 × 9 × 2 inches, and bake covered at 325° for 30 minutes, then uncover and bake 15 minutes longer. To add turkey flavor, baste with juices from the turkey roasting pan.

- Remove the stuffing from the turkey before carving and place in a separate container. Don't leave stuffing inside poultry because it doesn't cool quickly enough, which can allow bacteria to grow more easily.

- If you decide not to stuff your turkey, you can add quartered onions and cloves of garlic to the cavity; or try wedges of lemon, orange and apples and fresh herbs.

Rice Stuffing

Prep: 20 min   **Cook:** 5 min

8 servings (1/2 cup each)

2 tablespoons butter
or margarine

1 medium stalk celery,
chopped (1/2 cup)

1 small onion, chopped
(1/4 cup)

1/2 teaspoon salt

1/8 teaspoon pepper

2 cups cooked rice

1/2 cup chopped walnuts

1/3 cup raisins

1/4 teaspoon paprika

4 slices bacon, crisply
cooked and crumbled

1 Melt butter in 10-inch skillet over medium-high heat. Cook celery, onion, salt and pepper in butter, stirring occasionally, until vegetables are tender; remove from heat.

2 Toss celery mixture and remaining ingredients. Use to stuff one 8- to 10-pound turkey. See Turkey Talk (page 14) for specific directions.

1 Serving: Calories 170 (Calories from Fat 80); Fat 9g (Saturated 3g); Cholesterol 10mg; Sodium 220mg; Carbohydrate 198 (Dietary Fiber 1g); Protein 4g. **Diet Exchanges:** 1 Starch, 2 Fat.

Wild Rice–Pecan Stuffing: Substitute 1 cup cooked wild rice for 1 cup of the cooked rice and substitute pecans for the walnuts. Omit raisins and paprika. To cook wild rice, heat 1/3 cup uncooked wild rice and 1 cup water to boiling, reduce heat to low and simmer about 40 minutes or until water is absorbed.

Betty's Do-Ahead

This stuffing goes together quickly if the rice is cooked ahead of time. Cook rice according to package directions and refrigerate, covered, for up to 5 days.

Vegetable–Herb Stuffing

Prep: 45 min   Cook: 5 min   **10 servings (1/2 cup each)**

**2 tablespoons butter
or margarine**

**2 medium stalks celery,
sliced (1 cup)**

**1 medium onion,
chopped (1/2 cup)**

**1/4 cup chopped
fresh parsley**

**1 tablespoon chopped
fresh or 1 teaspoon dried
sage leaves**

**1 1/2 teaspoons chopped
fresh or 1/2 teaspoon
dried marjoram leaves**

**3/4 teaspoon chopped
fresh or 1/4 teaspoon
dried tarragon leaves**

1/2 teaspoon salt

**7 cups soft bread cubes
(about 10 slices bread)**

**2 medium carrots,
shredded (1 1/2 cups)**

**1 medium zucchini,
shredded (1 cup)**

**1 cup chopped fresh
mushrooms (4 ounces)**

1 Melt butter in 10-inch nonstick skillet over medium heat. Cook celery and onion in butter, stirring frequently, until onion is tender. Stir in parsley, sage, marjoram, tarragon and salt.

2 Mix bread cubes, carrots, zucchini and mushrooms in large bowl. Add celery mixture; toss. Use to stuff one 10- to 12-pound turkey. See Turkey Talk (page 14) for specific directions.

1 Serving: Calories 105 (Calories from Fat 25); Fat 3g (Saturated 2g); Cholesterol 5mg; Sodium 280mg; Carbohydrate 16g (Dietary Fiber 2g); Protein 3g. **Diet Exchanges:** 1 Starch, 1/2 Fat.

Betty's Simple Substitution

Try this new twist on stuffing made with vegetables. Use whatever vegetables and herbs you have on hand. Add bell peppers, sweet potato shreds or yellow summer squash in place of the celery, carrots and zucchini.

Slow Cooker Chorizo, Pecan and Cheddar Stuffing

Prep: 15 min   **Cook:** 3 hr 30 min   **16 servings (1/2 cup each)**

(see photo insert)

1 pound chorizo sausage, casing removed and crumbled, or bulk chorizo sausage

1 large onion, chopped (1 cup)

3 medium stalks celery, sliced (1 1/2 cups)

1 package (16 ounces) seasoned corn bread stuffing crumbs (5 3/4 cups)

1/3 cup butter or margarine, melted

1/2 teaspoon rubbed sage

1/4 teaspoon pepper

2 cups chicken broth

1 1/2 cups shredded sharp Cheddar cheese (6 ounces)

1 cup pecan halves, toasted*

*To Toast Nuts: Bake uncovered in ungreased shallow pan in 350 ° oven about 10 minutes, stirring occasionally, until golden brown. Or cook in ungreased heavy skillet over medium-low heat 5 to 7 minutes, stirring frequently until browning begins, then stirring constantly until golden brown.

1 Cook sausage, onion and celery in 10-inch skillet over medium heat 8 to 10 minutes, stirring occasionally, until sausage is no longer pink; drain.

2 Place sausage mixture, stuffing crumbs, butter, sage and pepper in 4- to 5-quart slow cooker. Pour broth over mixture; toss to combine. Cover and cook on low heat setting 3 hours to 3 hours 30 minutes. Gently stir in cheese and pecans.

3 Serve or keep warm in slow cooker up to 1 hour. Or use this recipe to stuff Southwestern Turkey (page 23) or one 12- to 14-pound turkey. See Turkey Talk (page 14) for specific directions.

1 Serving: Calories 355 (Calories from Fat 215); Fat 24g (Saturated 9g); Cholesterol 45mg; Sodium 1030mg; Carbohydrate 24g (Dietary Fiber 2g); Protein 14g. **Diet Exchanges:** 1 1/2 Starch, 1 High-Fat Meat, 3 Fat.

Betty's Simple Substitution

Mild or spicy Italian sausage can be substituted for the uncooked chorizo sausage. The stuffing will have a less smoky flavor. Adjust seasoning with salt and pepper if needed.

Cranberry Stuffing

Prep: 20 min   **Cook:** 5 min

1 cup butter or margarine

3 medium stalks celery (with leaves), chopped (1 1/2 cups)

3/4 cup finely chopped onion

9 cups soft bread cubes (about 15 slices)

1/2 cup dried cranberries

2 tablespoons chopped fresh or 1 1/2 teaspoons dried sage leaves

1 tablespoon chopped fresh or 1 teaspoon dried thyme leaves

1 1/2 teaspoons salt

1/2 teaspoon pepper

1 Melt butter in 10-inch skillet over medium heat. Cook celery and onion in butter, stirring frequently, until onion is tender. Stir in about one-third of the bread cubes.

2 Place stuffing mixture in large bowl. Add remaining bread cubes and remaining ingredients; toss. Use to stuff one 10- to 12 pound turkey. See Turkey Talk (page 14) for specific directions.

1 **Serving:** Calories 160 (Calories from Fat 100); Fat 11g (Saturated 7g); Cholesterol 30mg; Sodium 380mg; Carbohydrate 14g (Dietary Fiber 1g); Protein 2g. **Diet Exchanges:** 1 Starch, 2 Fat.

Betty's Simple Substitution

You can vary the flavor of the stuffing by using other dried fruits in place of the dried cranberries. Try golden raisins, chopped prunes, dried cherries or dried blueberries.

Cajun Jambalaya Stuffing

Prep: 10 min   **Cook:** 33 min

12 servings (1/2 cup each)

1 package (8 ounces)
fat-free smoked turkey
sausage, diced

2 teaspoons vegetable oil

1 large onion, chopped
(1 cup)

1 small green bell pepper,
coarsely chopped
(2/3 cup)

1/4 cup finely chopped
fresh parsley

1 large clove garlic,
finely chopped

1 1/2 cups uncooked
long-grain white rice

1 can (10 1/2 ounces)
condensed chicken broth

1 1/3 cups water

1 teaspoon Cajun
seasoning for poultry

1 Cook sausage in 12-inch nonstick skillet over medium heat 3 to 5 minutes, stirring occasionally, until lightly browned. Remove sausage from skillet; set aside.

2 Add oil to same skillet; heat over medium-high heat. Cook onion, bell pepper, parsley and garlic in oil 3 to 5 minutes, stirring occasionally, until onion is tender. Stir in rice. Cook about 3 minutes, stirring occasionally, until rice is golden brown.

3 Stir in sausage, broth, water and Cajun seasoning. Heat to boiling; reduce heat to low. Cover and simmer 18 to 20 minutes or until rice is tender and liquid is absorbed. Use to stuff one 10- to 12-pound turkey. See Turkey Talk (page 14) for specific directions.

1 Serving: Calories 140 (Calories from Fat 25); Fat 3g (Saturated 1g); Cholesterol 10mg; Sodium 280mg; Carbohydrate 22g (Dietary Fiber 1g); Protein 6g. **Diet Exchanges:** 1 Starch, 1/2 Lean Meat, Vegetable.

Betty's Helpful Tip

Traditional Creole jambalaya, which combines spicy meat, vegetables and rice, makes a wonderful dressing or stuffing with a slightly hot bite. Use it to spice up Classic Roast Turkey (page 18), or serve it with Smoked Turkey (page 30) or Brined Whole Turkey (page 32).

Louisiana Favorites

Serves 12

Age-old cooking styles that come from this region, Creole and Cajun, are those of New Orleans and the Louisiana bayou country. From these shared traditions come two of the South's most endearing qualities, bountiful food and warm hospitality.

Cajun Deep-Fried Turkey, page 28
No-Drippings Gravy, page 49
Cajun Jambalaya Stuffing, above
Cranberry-Topped Sweet Potatoes, page 77
Apple-Cranberry Chutney, page 64
Bacon and Garlic Cheese Grits, page 88
Buttermilk Biscuits, page 119
Brandy Pecan Pie, page 165
Sweet Potato–Mallow Bars, page 175

Classic Cranberry Sauce

Prep: 15 min   **Cook:** 15 min   **Chill:** 3 hr   **About 4 cups sauce**

1 bag (12 ounces) fresh or frozen cranberries (about 3 1/2 cups)

2 cups sugar

2 cups water

1 Place cranberries in a strainer; rinse with cool water; remove any stems or blemished berries.

2 Heat sugar and water to boiling in 3-quart saucepan over medium heat, stirring occasionally. Boil 5 minutes.

3 Stir in cranberries. Heat to boiling over medium heat, stirring occasionally. Boil about 5 minutes, stirring occasionally, until cranberries begin to pop. Cover and refrigerate about 3 hours or until chilled.

1/4 Cup: Calories 110 (Calories from Fat 0); Fat 0g (Saturated 0g); Cholesterol 0mg; Sodium 0mg; Carbohydrate 29g (Dietary Fiber 1g); Protein 0g %. **Diet Exchanges:** 2 Fruit.

Cranberry-Orange Sauce: Use 1 bag (12 ounces) fresh or frozen cranberries (3 1/2 cups), 1 1/2 cups sugar and 1/2 cup water. Heat sugar and water to boiling in 2-quart saucepan over medium heat, stirring occasionally. Stir in cranberries and 2 teaspoons grated orange peel. Heat to boiling over medium heat, stirring occasionally. Boil about 5 minutes, stirring occasionally, until cranberries begin to pop. Cover and refrigerate about 3 hours or until chilled.

Betty's Do-Ahead

Be sure to cook the cranberries until they pop in order to release the natural pectin, which thickens the sauce. This sauce is a classic at Thanksgiving and is a great recipe to make several days ahead, as it's best served chilled. If desired, garnish with grated orange peel.

Ginger-Cranberry-Tangerine Sauce

Prep: 10 min   **Cook:** 1 min   **2 cups sauce**

1 can (16 ounces) whole berry cranberry sauce

3 tablespoons sweet orange marmalade

2 teaspoons grated gingerroot

1 clementine, peeled and sectioned

1 Heat cranberry sauce in 1-quart saucepan over low heat, stirring constantly, until melted. Stir in marmalade, gingerroot and clementine sections. Cook 1 minute.

2 Serve sauce warm or cool.

1 **Serving:** Calories 110 (Calories from Fat 0); Fat 0g (Saturated 0g); Cholesterol 0mg; Sodium 15mg; Carbohydrate 28g (Dietary Fiber 1g); Protein 0g. **Diet Exchanges:** 2 Fruit.

Betty's Simple Substitution

You can use half of an 11-ounce can of mandarin orange segments, drained, instead of the clementine.

Northeast Favorites

Serves 12

It is in New England that some of our traditional cooking developed as the Pilgrims learned from the Native Americans how to grow corn, beans, pumpkin and squash. The colonists were introduced to such native produce as wild blueberries, cranberries, chestnuts and maple syrup. Few of these recipes would be recognizable today by the original settlers; as often happens, recipes have a way of evolving over the years.

Oyster Stew, page 129
Savory Apple-Onion Turkey, page 20
Apple Cider Gravy, page 21
Ginger-Cranberry-Tangerine Sauce, above
Oyster Stuffing or Chestnut Stuffing, page 52
Mashed Maple Sweet Potatoes, page 76
Classic Dinner Rolls, page 112
Sweet Maple Maize Pudding, page 168
Apple-Mince Streusel Pie, page 162

Cranberry-Orange Relish

Prep: 20 min   **Chill:** 24 hr

About 2 1/2 cups relish

1 bag (12 ounces) fresh or frozen cranberries (3 1/2 cups)

1 unpeeled orange

1 cup sugar

1 tablespoon finely chopped crystallized ginger, if desired

1 Place cranberries in a strainer; rinse with cool water; remove any stems or blemished berries. Wash and dry orange; cut into 1-inch pieces (with peel) and remove seeds.

2 Place sugar and ginger in medium bowl.

3 Place half each of the cranberries and orange pieces in food processor. Cover and process, using short on-and-off motions, about 15 seconds or until evenly chopped. Stir processed cranberry-orange mixture into sugar mixture. Repeat with remaining cranberries and orange pieces. Cover and refrigerate at least 24 hours to blend flavors but no longer than 1 week.

1/4 Cup: Calories 105 (Calories from Fat 0); Fat 0g (Saturated 0g); Cholesterol 0mg; Sodium 0mg; Carbohydrate 25g (Dietary Fiber 2g); Protein 0g. **Diet Exchanges:** 1 1/2 Fruit.

Betty's Helpful Tip

If you love the taste of ginger, use a 1/2-inch to 1-inch piece of crystallized ginger and place in food processor with the sugar. Process until ginger is finely chopped and transfer to a bowl. Then chop the cranberries and orange in the processor. This relish is a natural with turkey, chicken, ham or any pork recipe.

Tangy Cherry Sauce

Prep: 10 min   **Cook:** 8 min   **2 cups sauce**

1/2 cup packed brown sugar

2 tablespoons cornstarch

1 teaspoon ground mustard

1 cup dried sour cherries

1 1/2 cups water

1 teaspoon grated lemon peel

1/4 cup lemon juice

1 Mix brown sugar, cornstarch and mustard in 2 1/2-quart saucepan. Stir in remaining ingredients. Cook over low heat 6 to 8 minutes, stirring constantly, until thickened.

2 Serve sauce with turkey, chicken or pork, or use to glaze a 10- to 12-pound ham.

1/4 Cup: Calories 110 (Calories from Fat 0); Fat 0g (Saturated 0g); Cholesterol 0mg; Sodium 10mg; Carbohydrate 28g (Dietary Fiber 1g); Protein 0g. **Diet Exchanges:** 2 Fruit.

Betty's Do-Ahead

Make Tangy Cherry Sauce ahead of time and reheat in the microwave at serving time. Place in microwavable bowl and microwave loosely covered on High 1 minute; stir. Microwave 30 seconds longer or until heated through.

Southwest Favorites

Serves 15

The cooking of the Southwest mirrors the contrasting cultures in rich and flavorful combinations, influenced by the American Indians, Spanish, Mexicans and Anglo-Americans. The eating is hearty and heartfelt in this colorful region.

Southwestern Turkey, page 23
Slow Cooker Chorizo, Pecan and Cheddar Stuffing, page 56
Classic Pan Gravy, page 48
Tangy Cherry Sauce, above
Roasted Autumn Vegetables, page 82
Southern Buttermilk Corn Bread, page 123
Pumpkin Cheesecake, page 158 or No-Crust Harvest Pumpkin Pie, page 156
Cranberry-Raspberry Bread Pudding, page 167

Spicy Fruit Compote

Prep: 10 min   **Cook:** 15 min   **Stand:** 10 min   **3 cups compote**

1 cup orange juice

1/2 cup water

1/3 cup maple-flavored syrup or packed brown sugar

1/2 cup sweetened dried cranberries

1/3 cup dried apricots, cut in half

2 pears or apples, peeled and cut into bite-size pieces

2 tablespoons sugar

1/4 teaspoon pumpkin pie spice

2 cinnamon sticks

1 Mix all ingredients in 2-quart saucepan until blended. Heat to boiling over medium-high heat; reduce heat to low. Simmer uncovered 8 to 12 minutes or until pears are tender.

2 Let stand at room temperature 10 minutes. Remove cinnamon sticks. Serve compote warm or cold.

1 **Serving:** Calories 70 (Calories from Fat 0); Fat 0g (Saturated 0g); Cholesterol 0mg; Sodium 0mg; Carbohydrate 18g (Dietary Fiber 1g); Protein 0g. **Diet Exchanges:** 1 Fruit.

Betty's Do-Ahead

This colorful mixture of fresh and dried fruits sweetened with maple syrup can be made up to 4 days ahead of time; cover and refrigerate. Serve cold, or reheat in the microwave on High 1 to 2 minutes until warm.

Apple-Cranberry Chutney

Prep: 10 min   **Cook:** 1 hr

(see photo insert)

2 cups chutney

**2 cups fresh or frozen
cranberries**

**2 medium apples,
chopped (2 cups)**

**1 medium red bell pepper,
chopped (1 cup)**

**1 small onion, finely
chopped (1/4 cup)**

**3/4 cup packed
brown sugar**

1/2 cup golden raisins

1/2 cup white vinegar

**1 1/2 teaspoons finely
chopped gingerroot**

**1 clove garlic, finely
chopped**

1 Place cranberries in a strainer; rinse with cool water; remove any stems
or blemished berries.

2 Mix cranberries and remaining ingredients in 2-quart saucepan. Heat to
boiling, stirring frequently; reduce heat to low.

3 Simmer uncovered about 1 hour, stirring frequently, until mixture thickens and fruits are tender. Store covered in nonaluminum container in
refrigerator up to 2 weeks. Serve chutney with roast turkey, ham or pork.

1/4 Cup: Calories 150 (Calories from Fat 0); Fat 0g (Saturated 0g); Cholesterol 0mg; Sodium 10mg;
Carbohydrate 39g (Dietary Fiber 3g); Protein 1g. **Diet Exchanges:** 2 1/2 Fruit.

Betty's Do-Ahead

To store chutney for a
longer time, pour hot
chutney into hot, steril-
ized jars, leaving 1/4-inch
headspace. Wipe rims of
jars, then seal and cool
on a wire rack for 1 hour.
Chutney can be stored in
the refrigerator for up to
2 months, so it's a great
idea for a hostess gift.

Cranberry-Apple Glazed Turkey (page 19)

Butter- and Wine-Basted
Turkey Breast (page 35)

Slow Cooker Chorizo, Pecan and Cheddar Stuffing (page 56)

Apple-Cranberry Chutney (page 64)

Easy Mashed Potato Casserole (page 72)

Slow Cooker Sweet Potatoes (page 79)

Fall Harvest Squash (page 81)

Creamy Confetti Succotash (page 85)

Cranberry Applesauce

Prep: 10 min   **Cook:** 15 min

2 1/4 cups applesauce

2 cups fresh or frozen cranberries

2 medium peeled or unpeeled apples (Braeburn, Golden Delicious or McIntosh), sliced

3/4 cup water

1 cup sugar

1 Place cranberries in a strainer; rinse with cool water; remove any stems or blemished berries.

2 Heat cranberries, apples and water to boiling in 2-quart saucepan over medium-high heat; reduce heat. Simmer uncovered about 10 minutes or until cranberries and apples are soft. Stir in sugar. Cook 1 to 2 minutes, stirring occasionally, until sugar is dissolved.

3 For chunky applesauce, serve as is. For smooth applesauce, process mixture in food processor 15 to 30 seconds.

1/4 Cup: Calories 115 (Calories from Fat 0); Fat 0g (Saturated 0g); Cholesterol 0mg; Sodium 0mg; Carbohydrate 29g (Dietary Fiber 2g); Protein 0g. **Diet Exchanges:** 2 Fruit.

Betty's Simple Substitution

For an incredibly easy no-cook sauce, stir together a 16-ounce can of whole berry cranberry sauce and 1 cup of applesauce.

Sensational Sides

Turkey Dinner Time-Savers

You've heard it before: You can save time in the end by starting ahead. Consult the recipes in this cookbook that you're planning to prepare for do-ahead information and tips. Here are some real keepers: dishes you can get started on or even make completely a few days or up to a week ahead.

- **Dips, spreads and cheese balls:** Make them a day or two ahead; cover tightly and refrigerate.
- **Relish dish:** Assemble olives, pickles, radishes, carrot and celery sticks in the serving dish 2 days ahead; cover and refrigerate.
- **Vegetables for dipping:** Cut them up 2 days ahead; put in plastic storage bags and refrigerate.
- **Ready-to-go turkey:** Buy a fresh turkey this year or start thawing your frozen turkey at least 3 days ahead so it can thaw in the refrigerator.
- **Stuffing:** Stir together the ingredients the day before; cover tightly and refrigerate. (Don't stuff turkey ahead of time.)
- **Slow cooker stuffing:** Mix ingredients and start cooking stuffing in the morning; it can cook all day unattended.
- **Mashed potatoes:** Cook and mash potatoes 1 or 2 days ahead. Wrap tightly in plastic wrap or place in a tightly covered microwavable dish and refrigerate.
- **Twice-baked potatoes:** Fill the skins a week or more ahead, sprinkle with cheese, wrap tightly and freeze. Pop them in the oven to bake.
- **Candied sweet potatoes:** Cook potatoes the day before. Cover tightly and refrigerate.
- **Cranberry sauce:** Make it from scratch, following your recipe or directions on the package; cover and refrigerate up to 1 week.
- **Dinner rolls or biscuits:** Bake up to 2 weeks ahead and cool completely. Place in covered container and freeze. Thaw and warm right before serving.
- **Fruit pie:** Bake ahead and either refrigerate or freeze.
- **Pumpkin pie:** Bake the day before, cover and refrigerate.

Classic Green Bean Casserole

Prep: 10 min   **Bake:** 40 min

6 servings

1 can (10 3/4 ounces)
**condensed cream of
mushroom, cream
of celery or cream
of chicken soup**

1/2 cup milk

1/8 teaspoon pepper

**2 cans (14 1/2 ounces
each) French-style green
beans, drained**

**1 can (2.8 ounces)
French-fried onions**

1 Heat oven to 375°. Mix soup, milk and pepper in 2-quart casserole or
square baking dish, 8 × 8 × 2 inches. Stir in beans. Sprinkle with onions.

2 Bake uncovered 30 to 40 minutes or until hot in center.

1 Serving (about 3/4 cup): Calories 170 (Calories from Fat 90); Fat 10g (Saturated 2g); Cholesterol 5mg; Sodium 840mg;
Carbohydrate 16g (Dietary Fiber 3g); Protein 4g. **Diet Exchanges:** 1/2 Starch, 2 Vegetable, 1 1/2 Fat.

Betty's Simple Substitution

To use frozen green beans
in this family favorite,
cook 2 bags (1 pound
each) frozen cut green
beans as directed on the
bag for the minimum
time, then drain and
follow this recipe.

Easy Green Beans and Cranberries

Prep: 5 min   **Cook:** 15 min

4 servings

1 bag (1 pound) frozen cut green beans

1 teaspoon grated orange peel

1/2 cup dried cranberries

2 tablespoons honey

1/4 cup bacon flavor bits or chips

1 Cook beans as directed on bag, adding orange peel before cooking; drain.

2 Stir in cranberries and honey. Top with bacon bits.

1 Serving: Calories 145 (Calories from Fat 10); Fat 1g (Saturated 0g); Cholesterol 0mg; Sodium 140mg; Carbohydrate 30g (Dietary Fiber 4g); Protein 5g. **Diet Exchanges:** 3 Vegetable, 1 Fruit.

Betty's Helpful Tip

Try other frozen vegetables prepared this festive yet easy way. Good choices are broccoli, cauliflower, carrots or a combination of the three.

Classic Mashed Potatoes

Prep: 20 min   **Cook:** 35 min

4 to 6 servings

6 medium red or white potatoes (2 pounds), peeled and cut into small pieces

1/3 to 1/2 cup milk, warmed

1/4 cup butter or margarine, softened

1/2 teaspoon salt

Dash of pepper

1 Place potatoes in 2-quart saucepan; add enough water just to cover potatoes. Heat to boiling; reduce heat. Cover and cook 20 to 25 minutes or until potatoes are tender when pierced with a fork. (Cooking time will vary, depending on size of potato pieces and type of potato used.) Drain potatoes in strainer.

2 Return potatoes to saucepan. Heat potatoes over low heat about 1 minute, shaking pan often to keep potatoes from sticking and burning, to dry potatoes (this will help make mashed potatoes fluffier).

3 Mash potatoes in pan with potato masher or electric mixer on low speed 1 to 2 minutes or until no lumps remain. Add milk in small amounts, beating after each addition. (Amount of milk needed to make potatoes smooth and fluffy depends on type of potatoes used.) Add butter, salt and pepper. Mash vigorously until potatoes are light and fluffy.

1 Serving: Calories 275 (Calories from Fat 110); Fat 12g (Saturated 7g); Cholesterol 30mg; Sodium 390mg; Carbohydrate 38g (Dietary Fiber 3g); Protein 4g. **Diet Exchanges:** 1 1/2 Starch, 1 Fruit, 3 Fat.

Do-Ahead Mashed Potatoes: To prepare these potatoes a day ahead of time, follow directions through step 3. Spray inside of 1 1/2-quart casserole with cooking spray. Spoon mashed potatoes into casserole; cover and refrigerate up to 24 hours. To reheat, microwave uncovered on High 4 to 5 minutes or until hot. Stir potatoes before serving.

Garlic Mashed Potatoes: Cook 6 cloves garlic, peeled, with the potatoes.

Betty's Helpful Tip

Warming the milk and softening the butter before you add them to the potatoes will give you smoother mashed potatoes; and they'll stay warmer longer when you bring them to the table.

Easy Mashed Potato Casserole

Prep: 15 min   **Bake:** 30 min   **8 servings**

(see photo insert)

**2 teaspoons butter
or margarine**

**16 medium green onions,
sliced (1 cup)**

**1 medium yellow or
orange bell pepper,
chopped (1 cup)**

3 cups hot water

**1 cup half-and-half
or whole milk**

**1/4 cup butter or
margarine**

**1 package (3.8 ounces)
roasted garlic mashed
potatoes (2 packets)**

**1 1/2 cups shredded
Cheddar cheese (6 ounces)**

1 Heat oven to 350°. Grease bottom and side of 1-quart casserole with shortening. Melt 2 teaspoons butter in 8-inch nonstick skillet over medium-high heat. Cook onions and bell pepper in butter 1 minute, stirring occasionally. Remove from heat; set aside.

2 Heat water, half-and-half and 1/4 cup butter to boiling in 2-quart saucepan; remove from heat. Stir in both packets of potatoes (and seasoning) just until moistened. Let stand about 1 minute or until liquid is absorbed. Beat with fork until smooth.

3 Spoon 1 1/3 cups of the potatoes into casserole; top with half of the onion mixture and 3/4 cup of the cheese. Spoon another 1 1/3 cups potatoes over cheese; carefully spread to cover. Sprinkle evenly with remaining onion mixture. Top with remaining potatoes; carefully spread to cover. Sprinkle with remaining 3/4 cup cheese.

4 Bake uncovered about 30 minutes or until hot.

1 Serving: Calories 295 (Calories from Fat 155); Fat 17g (Saturated 11g); Cholesterol 50mg; Sodium 210mg; Carbohydrate 26g (Dietary Fiber 3g); Protein 9g. **Diet Exchanges:** 2 Starch, 3 Fat.

Betty's Do-Ahead

The whole family will love this tasty side dish. Make it up to 24 hours ahead of time, following directions through step 3, then cover and refrigerate up to 24 hours. Bake about 45 minutes or until hot.

Grilled Smoky Cheddar Potatoes

Prep: 10 min   **Grill:** 1 hr

6 servings

6 medium potatoes, cut into 1-inch chunks

1/2 teaspoon salt

2 tablespoons butter or margarine

1 cup shredded Cheddar cheese (4 ounces)

2 tablespoons bacon flavor bits or chips

2 medium green onions, sliced (2 tablespoons)

1 Heat coals or gas grill for direct heat. Place potatoes on 30 × 18-inch piece of heavy-duty aluminum foil. Sprinkle salt over potatoes. Cut butter into small pieces; sprinkle over potatoes. Sprinkle with cheese and bacon bits.

2 Wrap foil securely around potatoes. Pierce top of foil once or twice with fork to vent steam.

3 Cover and grill foil packet, seam side up, 4 to 6 inches from medium heat 45 to 60 minutes or until potatoes are tender. Sprinkle with onions.

1 Serving: Calories 220 (Calories from Fat 100); Fat 11g (Saturated 6g); Cholesterol 30mg; Sodium 390mg; Carbohydrate 22g (Dietary Fiber 2g); Protein 8g. **Diet Exchanges:** 1 1/2 Starch, 2 Fat.

Betty's Simple Substitution

Here's a side that doesn't take up oven or stovetop space. Try Yukon gold potatoes for a pretty color and rich, buttery taste. And for extra-smoky potatoes, use smoked Cheddar cheese. Or, if you've got the grill fired up for the turkey, use it for your side dish, too.

Bountiful Twice-Baked Potatoes

Prep: 20 min   **Bake:** 1 hr 50 min

6 servings

**3 large baking potatoes
(1 pound)**

**3 large dark-orange
sweet potatoes (1 pound)**

3 tablespoons milk

**2 tablespoons butter
or margarine, softened**

1/4 teaspoon salt

1/8 teaspoon pepper

**2 tablespoons
maple-flavored syrup**

**2 tablespoons butter
or margarine, softened**

1 Heat oven to 350°. Pierce baking potatoes and sweet potatoes several times with fork to allow steam to escape. Bake 1 hour 15 minutes to 1 hour 30 minutes or until tender when pierced with a fork.

2 Cut baking potatoes lengthwise in half; scoop out insides, leaving a thin shell. Mash potatoes in medium bowl with electric mixer on low speed until no lumps remain. Add milk in small amounts, beating after each addition. (Amount of milk needed to make potatoes smooth and fluffy depends on type of potatoes used.) Add 2 tablespoons butter, the salt and pepper; beat vigorously until potatoes are light and fluffy. Fill half of the potato shells with mashed potatoes.

3 Peel sweet potatoes; mash in medium bowl. Stir in maple syrup and 2 tablespoons butter. Fill remaining potato shells with mashed sweet potatoes.

4 Increase oven temperature to 400°. Bake potatoes on ungreased cookie sheet about 20 minutes or until hot.

1 Serving: Calories 290 (Calories from Fat 100); Fat 11g (Saturated 6g); Cholesterol 30mg; Sodium 190mg; Carbohydrate 44g (Dietary Fiber 4g); Protein 3g. **Diet Exchanges:** 1 Starch, 2 Fruit, 2 Fat.

Betty's Do-Ahead

To prepare these potatoes ahead of time, follow directions through step 3. Tightly cover and refrigerate filled potatoes up to 48 hours. About 40 minutes before serving, heat oven to 400°. Uncover and bake on ungreased cookie sheet about 30 minutes or until hot.

Or to freeze, place filled potatoes in airtight freezer container and freeze up to 2 months. About 50 minutes before serving, heat oven to 400°. Bake uncovered on ungreased cookie sheet about 40 minutes or until hot.

Classic Sweet Potatoes with Marshmallows

Prep: 20 min   **Cook:** 35 min   **Bake:** 30 min   **8 servings (1/2 cup each)**

6 medium dark-orange sweet potatoes (2 pounds)

1/3 cup packed brown sugar

2 tablespoons butter or margarine, melted

15 to 20 large marshmallows or 2 cups miniature marshmallow

1 Place potatoes in 3-quart saucepan; add enough water just to cover potatoes. Heat to boiling; reduce heat. Cover and simmer 20 to 25 minutes or until potatoes are tender when pierced with a fork; drain. (If desired, save the water used to boil the sweet potatoes to use in gravy.) When potatoes are cool enough to handle, slip off skins; cut potatoes into 1/2-inch slices.

2 Heat oven to 325°. Spray square baking dish, 8 × 8 × 2 inches, with cooking spray. Place potatoes in baking dish. Sprinkle with brown sugar; drizzle with butter.

3 Bake uncovered 20 to 25 minutes or until thoroughly heated and edges are bubbly; remove from oven. Top with marshmallows. Bake uncovered 4 to 5 minutes longer or until marshmallows are puffed and just starting to brown.

1 Serving: Calories 255 (Calories from Fat 35); Fat 4g (Saturated 2g); Cholesterol 10mg; Sodium 50mg; Carbohydrate 53g (Dietary Fiber 3g); Protein 2g. **Diet Exchanges:** 1 Starch, 2 1/2 Fruit, 1/2 Fat.

Betty's Simple Substitution

Instead of starting with your own sweet potatoes, you can use canned sweet potatoes. Use two 23-ounce cans of sweet potatoes, and begin the recipe with step 2.

Mashed Maple Sweet Potatoes

Prep: 15 min   **Bake:** 1 hr 15 min   **6 servings**

**3 pounds red garnet
or dark-orange sweet
potatoes**

**2 tablespoons
maple-flavored syrup**

**2 tablespoons butter
or margarine, softened**

1/2 teaspoon salt

Ground nutmeg to taste

**Additional maple-flavored
syrup, if desired**

**1/4 cup chopped pecans,
toasted*, if desired**

*To Toast Nuts: Bake uncovered in
ungreased shallow pan in 350° oven
about 10 minutes, stirring occasionally,
until golden brown. Or cook in ungreased heavy skillet over medium-low
heat 5 to 7 minutes, stirring frequently
until browning begins, then stirring
constantly until golden brown.

1 Heat oven to 350°. Pierce potatoes with fork. Place potatoes in square pan, 9 × 9 × 2 inches. Cover and bake about 1 hour 15 minutes or until potatoes are tender when pierced with a fork.

2 When potatoes are cool enough to handle, slip off skins. Mash potatoes in medium bowl with electric mixer on medium speed until no lumps remain. Add 2 tablespoons maple syrup, the butter, salt and nutmeg. Continue beating until potatoes are light and fluffy. Drizzle with additional syrup and sprinkle with pecans.

1 Serving: Calories 195 (Calories from Fat 35); Fat 4g (Saturated 1g); Cholesterol 0mg; Sodium 240mg; Carbohydrate 38g (Dietary Fiber 4g); Protein 2g. **Diet Exchanges:** 1 Starch, 1 1/2 Fruit, 1/2 Fat.

Betty's Do-Ahead

To make ahead of time, cover and refrigerate mashed sweet potatoes up to 24 hours, then reheat in the microwave oven or a slow cooker on low heat setting until warm.

All About
Sweet Potatoes or Yams

Q. **What's the difference?**

A. At the supermarket you may find a flavorful variety of sweet potato, with copper-colored skin and deep orange flesh, which is often labeled as ruby or garnet yam. True yams are another vegetable altogether and are rarely found in America. When buying sweet potatoes, choose firm, smooth-skinned potatoes without soft spots, cracks or blemishes. Sweet potatoes were growing in the New World when the Pilgrims arrived, and today they are present in some form on most American Thanksgiving tables. For a different taste treat, cooked sweet potatoes are combined with eggs, milk and spices and baked in Sweet Potato Pie (page 159).

Cranberry-Topped Sweet Potatoes

Prep: 15 min   **Cook:** 30 min   **Bake:** 30 min   **8 servings**

6 medium dark-orange sweet potatoes (2 pounds), peeled and cut into small pieces

2 tablespoons butter or margarine

1/2 teaspoon salt

1/2 cup soft bread crumbs (about 1 slice bread)

1/4 cup dried cranberries

1/4 cup coarsely chopped pecans

2 tablespoons butter or margarine, melted

1 Place sweet potatoes in 3-quart saucepan; add enough water just to cover potatoes. Cover and heat to boiling; reduce heat. Simmer covered 20 to 25 minutes or until potatoes are tender when pierced with a fork; drain. Return potatoes to saucepan. Heat potatoes over low heat about 1 minute, shaking pan often to keep potatoes from sticking and burning, to dry potatoes.

2 Heat oven to 350°. Mash potatoes, 2 tablespoons butter and the salt in medium bowl with potato masher or electric mixer on low speed until no lumps remain. Spoon into ungreased 1-quart casserole. Mix remaining ingredients; sprinkle over potatoes.

3 Bake uncovered about 30 minutes or until potatoes are hot and topping mixture is golden brown.

1 Serving: Calories 195 (Calories from Fat 80); Fat 9g (Saturated 4g); Cholesterol 15mg; Sodium 210mg; Carbohydrate 26g (Dietary Fiber 3g); Protein 2g. **Diet Exchanges:** 1 Starch, 1 Fruit, 1 Fat.

Betty's Do-Ahead

You can make these super potatoes a day ahead. Just follow the directions through step 2, then cover and refrigerate up to 24 hours. Bake uncovered 45 to 60 minutes or until potatoes are hot and topping mixture is golden brown.

Oven-Roasted Sweet Potatoes

Prep: 10 min   **Bake:** 30 min   **8 servings**

**4 large dark-orange
sweet potatoes (3 pounds)**

**1 tablespoon olive
or vegetable oil**

2 tablespoons honey

**1/2 teaspoon dried
rosemary leaves,
crumbled**

1/4 teaspoon salt

1 Heat oven to 425°. Grease bottom and sides of jelly roll pan, 15 1/2 ×
10 1/2 × 1 inch, with shortening. Peel sweet potatoes; cut crosswise into
3/4-inch slices, halving larger sweet potatoes if necessary. Place potatoes
in single layer in pan.

2 Mix remaining ingredients in small microwavable bowl. Microwave
uncovered on High 20 to 30 seconds or until hot. Stir oil mixture;
brush over potato slices.

3 Bake uncovered 25 to 30 minutes or until potatoes are tender.

1 Serving: Calories 130 (Calories from Fat 20); Fat 2g (Saturated 0g); Cholesterol 0mg; Sodium 80mg;
Carbohydrate 26g (Dietary Fiber 3g); Protein 2g. **Diet Exchanges:** 1 Starch, 1 Fruit.

*Betty's
Helpful Tip*

A variety of sweet pota-
toes with dark orange
skin is often labeled as
"yam," in the supermarket.
In the Betty Crocker test
kitchens, the darker sweet
potatoes (or "yams") are
a favorite for this dish.
The very light-colored
sweet potatoes are not as
sweet and are drier than
the darker-skinned ones.

Low-Fat Thanksgiving Dinner

Serves 4

Low-fat cooking doesn't have to mean sacrificing flavor or that the
food will be any less satisfying. It just means that your guests will be
eating a more healthful dinner, including lots of veggies, perhaps a fruit
for dessert and smaller servings.

Citrus Fruit Salad, page 144
Rosemary-Lemon Roasted Turkey, page 22
Vegetable-Herb Stuffing, page 55
Baked Potatoes or Oven-Roasted Sweet Potatoes, above
Thin Gravy (smaller serving), page 48
Cranberry Applesauce, page 65
Bread Machine Blueberry Corn Bread, page 113
Cranberry Herbal Tea Granita, page 178
Slow Cooker Maple-Sauced Pears, page 176
Coffee, tea and wine, if desired

Slow Cooker Sweet Potatoes

Prep: 15 min   **Cook:** 8 hr

(see photo insert)

10 servings

6 medium dark-orange sweet potatoes (2 pounds)

1 1/2 cups applesauce

1/2 cup packed brown sugar

3 tablespoons butter or margarine, melted

1 teaspoon ground cinnamon

1/2 cup chopped nuts

1 Peel sweet potatoes; cut into 1/2-inch cubes. Place potatoes in 2- to 3 1/2-quart slow cooker. Mix remaining ingredients except nuts; spoon over potatoes.

2 Cover and cook on low heat setting 6 to 8 hours or until potatoes are very tender.

3 Meanwhile, cook nuts in ungreased heavy skillet over medium-low heat 5 to 7 minutes, stirring frequently until browning begins, then stirring constantly until golden brown; set aside. Sprinkle nuts over sweet potatoes.

1 Serving: Calories 245 (Calories from Fat 70); Fat 8g (Saturated 3g); Cholesterol 10mg; Sodium 40mg; Carbohydrate 41g (Dietary Fiber 4g); Protein 2g. **Diet Exchanges:** 1 Starch, 2 Fruit, 1 Fat.

Betty's Helpful Tip

While the turkey roasts in the oven, cook this Thanksgiving favorite in the slow cooker. If your home is the holiday gathering spot for family and friends, you can double or triple this recipe and cook it in a 5- to 6-quart slow cooker.

Butternut Squash Sauté

Prep: 20 min   **Cook:** 20 min   **8 servings**

**4 slices bacon, cut into
1-inch pieces**

**1 medium onion,
chopped (1/2 cup)**

**2 small butternut squash,
peeled and cut into
1/2-inch pieces (6 cups)**

**1/2 teaspoon chopped
fresh or 1/8 teaspoon
dried thyme leaves**

1/8 teaspoon pepper

**3 cups firmly packed
baby spinach leaves**

1 Cook bacon in 12-inch skillet over medium-low heat, stirring occasionally, until crisp. Stir in onion. Cook about 2 minutes, stirring occasionally, until onion is crisp-tender.

2 Stir in squash, thyme and pepper. Cover and cook 8 to 10 minutes, stirring occasionally, until squash is tender. Stir in spinach just until wilted.

1 **Serving:** Calories 80 (Calories from Fat 20); Fat 2g (Saturated 1g); Cholesterol 5mg; Sodium 65mg; Carbohydrate 13g (Dietary Fiber 2g); Protein 2g. **Diet Exchanges:** 2 Vegetable, 1/2 Fat.

Betty's Helpful Tip

If you need to make a larger quantity, here's how. For 12 servings, use 6 slices bacon, 2/3 cup chopped onion, 9 cups cut-up squash, 3/4 teaspoon fresh or 1/4 teaspoon dried thyme leaves, 1/4 teaspoon pepper and 4 1/2 cups spinach leaves. Make in a 4-quart Dutch oven.

Delicious Diabetes Dinner

Serves 8 to 10

If a family member or friend with diabetes is coming for dinner, your Thanksgiving meal may need a little altering. Serve a relish tray (page 127) and more than one vegetable or a plain salad and vegetable. Select recipes without a lot of added ingredients (vegetable or lettuce salads with dips or dressings on the side are ideal). Offer smaller servings and suggest a walk after dinner to lower blood sugar. This dinner contains four or five Carbohydrate Choices, with choice of dessert served later.

Festive Fall Coleslaw, page 141
Rosemary-Lemon Roasted Turkey, page 22
Vegetable-Herb Stuffing, page 55
Vegetable Juice Gravy, page 48
Spicy Fruit Compote, page 63
Butternut Squash Sauté, above
Impossibly Easy Pumpkin Pie, page 157
White Chocolate Chunk–Cranberry Cookies, page 173
or Spicy Pumpkin Drop Cookies, page 174
Water, Coffee and Tea

Fall Harvest Squash

Prep: 15 min   **Bake:** 1 hr

(see photo insert)

**1 buttercup squash
(2 to 2 1/2 pounds)**

**2 tablespoons butter
or margarine, melted**

**2 tablespoons peach
or apricot preserves**

**2 tablespoons graham
cracker crumbs**

**2 tablespoons shredded
coconut**

**1/4 teaspoon
ground ginger**

**1/8 teaspoon
ground allspice**

1/8 teaspoon pepper

1 Heat oven to 350°. Cut squash into fourths; remove seeds and fibers. Place squash, cut sides up, in ungreased rectangular pan, 13 × 9 × 2 inches.

2 Mix butter and preserves. Brush about half of preserves mixture over cut sides of squash pieces. Mix remaining ingredients; sprinkle over squash. Drizzle with remaining preserves mixture.

3 Bake uncovered 45 to 60 minutes or until tender.

1 Serving: Calories 180 (Calories from Fat 70); Fat 8g (Saturated 5g); Cholesterol 15mg; Sodium 65mg; Carbohydrate 25g (Dietary Fiber 5g); Protein 2g. **Diet Exchanges:** 1/2 Starch, 1 Fruit, 1 1/2 Fat.

Betty's Simple Substitution

Two acorn squash (1 to 1 1/2 pounds each) can be substituted for the buttercup squash. Grilled pork chops, pork roast and pork tenderloin are excellent choices to serve with this sweetly spiced squash.

Roasted Autumn Vegetables

Prep: 30 min   **Bake:** 30 min   **8 servings**

1/3 cup butter or margarine

1 tablespoon chopped fresh or 1 teaspoon dried sage leaves

2 cloves garlic, finely chopped

1 pound Brussels sprouts, cut in half

1 pound parsnips, peeled and cut into 2-inch pieces

1 bag (16 ounces) baby-cut carrots

1 small butternut squash, peeled, seeded and cut into 1-inch pieces

1 Heat oven to 375°. Melt butter in 1-quart saucepan; stir in sage and garlic. Place remaining ingredients in rectangular pan, 13 × 9 × 2 inches. Pour butter mixture over vegetables; stir to coat.

2 Cover and bake 25 to 30 minutes, stirring occasionally, until vegetables are crisp-tender.

1 Serving: Calories 175 (Calories from Fat 70); Fat 8g (Saturated 5g); Cholesterol 20mg; Sodium 90mg; Carbohydrate 28g (Dietary Fiber 7g); Protein 4g. **Diet Exchanges:** 2 Vegetable, 1 Fruit, 1 1/2 Fat.

Betty's Simple Substitution

You can use 2 medium Yukon gold potatoes, cut into eighths, in place of the butternut squash. Garnish with fresh sage leaves.

Classic Baked Corn Pudding

Prep: 20 min   **Bake:** 1 hr 5 min   **Stand:** 10 min   **16 servings (1/2 cup each)**

1/2 cup butter or margarine

1 small onion, chopped (1/4 cup)

1/2 cup all-purpose flour

1/2 teaspoon pepper

1/2 teaspoon salt

4 cups milk (1 quart)

6 eggs, slightly beaten

2 cups shredded Cheddar cheese (8 ounces)

6 cups frozen (thawed) whole kernel corn

1/2 cup chopped fresh parsley or 2 tablespoon parsley flakes

3/4 cup dry bread crumbs

3 tablespoons butter or margarine, melted

1 Heat oven to 350°. Grease bottom and sides of rectangular baking dish, 13 × 9 × 2 inches, or 3-quart casserole, with shortening, or spray with cooking spray.

2 Melt 1/2 cup butter in 4-quart Dutch oven over medium heat. Cook onion in butter 3 to 4 minutes, stirring constantly, until tender. Stir in flour, pepper and salt until well blended. Stir in milk. Cook 4 to 5 minutes, stirring constantly, until thickened. Gradually stir in eggs and cheese. Stir in corn and parsley. Pour into baking dish.

3 Mix bread crumbs and 3 tablespoons melted butter; sprinkle over corn mixture. Bake uncovered 55 to 65 minutes or until mixture is set and knife inserted in center comes out clean. Let stand 5 to 10 minutes before serving.

1 Serving: Calories 225 (Calories from Fat 115); Fat 13g (Saturated 8g); Cholesterol 95mg; Sodium 250mg; Carbohydrate 18g (Dietary Fiber 1g); Protein 9g. **Diet Exchanges:** 1 Starch, 1 Medium-Fat Meat, 1 1/2 Fat.

Betty's Simple Substitution

You can use a 15 1/4-ounce can of whole kernel corn, drained, instead of frozen corn.

Zesty Corn Combo

Prep: 10 min   **Cook:** 10 min   **8 servings**

1 tablespoon butter
or margarine

1 medium red bell pepper,
coarsely chopped (1 cup)

1 medium green bell
pepper, coarsely chopped
(1 cup)

1 medium jalapeño chili,
seeded and finely chopped

2 bags (1 pound each)
frozen whole kernel corn

2 teaspoons chopped
fresh or 1/2 teaspoon
dried oregano leaves

1/2 teaspoon salt

1/4 cup chopped fresh
cilantro

1 Melt butter in 12-inch nonstick skillet over medium heat. Cook bell peppers and chili in butter 2 to 3 minutes, stirring occasionally, until bell peppers are crisp-tender.

2 Stir in corn, oregano and salt. Cover and cook 5 to 6 minutes, stirring occasionally, until corn is tender. Stir in cilantro.

---

1 Serving: Calories 125 (Calories from Fat 20); Fat 2g (Saturated 1g); Cholesterol 0mg; Sodium 160mg; Carbohydrate 24g (Dietary Fiber 3g); Protein 3g. **Diet Exchanges:** 1 Starch, 2 Vegetable.

For 12 people: Use 2 tablespoons butter, 1 1/2 cups each chopped red and green bell peppers, 1 large jalapeño chili, 3 bags (1 pound each) corn, 1 tablespoon fresh or 3/4 teaspoon dried oregano leaves, 3/4 teaspoon salt and 1/3 cup cilantro. Make in a 4-quart Dutch oven.

Betty's Do-Ahead

Go easy on yourself the day of the feast by doing as much as you can ahead of time. Chop the peppers, chili and herbs ahead of time, and store in individual plastic food-storage bags in the refrigerator.

Creamy Confetti Succotash

Prep: 10 min   **Cook:** 10 min

5 servings

(see photo insert)

**1 tablespoon butter
or margarine**

**1 small yellow, orange,
red or green bell pepper,
chopped (1/2 cup)**

**2 medium green onions,
sliced (2 tablespoons)**

**2 cups fresh or frozen
whole kernel corn**

**1 cup frozen baby lima
beans**

1/4 cup half-and-half

**2 teaspoons chopped
fresh or 1/2 teaspoon
dried marjoram leaves**

1/4 teaspoon salt

1/8 teaspoon pepper

1 Melt butter in 10-inch skillet over medium-high heat. Cook bell pepper and onions in butter 2 to 3 minutes, stirring occasionally, until crisp-tender.

2 Stir in remaining ingredients; reduce heat to medium-low. Cover and cook 5 to 6 minutes, stirring occasionally, until vegetables are tender.

1 Serving: Calories 130 (Calories from Fat 35); Fat 4g (Saturated 2g); Cholesterol 10mg; Sodium 160mg; Carbohydrate 20g (Dietary Fiber 4g); Protein 4g. **Diet Exchanges:** 1 Starch, 1 Vegetable, 1/2 Fat.

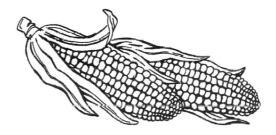

Betty's Helpful Tip

Add a festive, fall harvest look to your Thanksgiving dinner by using colorful seasonal vegetables and fruits, such as yellow and orange bell peppers.

Broccoli with Pine Nuts and Cranberry Relish

Prep: 12 min   **Cook:** 20 min   **6 servings**

1 1/2 pounds broccoli (stems and flowerets), cut into 2 × 1/2-inch pieces

1/2 teaspoon salt

1 cup fresh or frozen cranberries

1/2 cup packed brown sugar

1/4 cup water

1 tablespoon cider vinegar

1/4 teaspoon salt

1/8 teaspoon ground cinnamon

2 tablespoons pine nuts or slivered almonds

1 Heat 1 inch water to boiling in 3-quart saucepan. Add broccoli; reduce heat to low. Simmer uncovered 7 to 12 minutes or until tender; drain. Stir in salt.

2 Heat remaining ingredients except pine nuts to boiling in 1-quart saucepan; reduce heat to low. Cover and simmer 10 to 13 minutes, stirring occasionally, until most of the cranberries have popped and sauce has thickened.

3 Spread pine nuts in single layer in 8- or 10-inch skillet; cook and stir over medium-high heat 4 to 7 minutes or until lightly browned. Just before serving, spoon warm relish over broccoli; sprinkle with nuts.

1 Serving: Calories 140 (Calories from Fat 2); Fat 20g (Saturated 0g); Cholesterol 0mg; Sodium 330mg; Carbohydrate 26g (Dietary Fiber 4g); Protein 4g. **Diet Exchanges:** 1 Vegetable, 1 Fruit, 1/2 Fat.

Betty's Special Touch

You may toast the pine nuts ahead of time, but sprinkle them over the broccoli just before serving so they keep their crunch.

Easy Orange-Glazed Carrots

Prep: 12 min **Cook:** 8 min 6 servings

1 bag (16 ounces) baby-cut carrots

1/4 cup slivered almonds

1/3 cup orange marmalade

1/2 cup golden raisins

1 Heat 1/2 cup water to boiling in 1 1/2- to 2-quart saucepan. Add carrots. Heat to boiling; reduce heat to medium. Cover and cook 10 to 12 minutes, stirring occasionally, until tender.

2 While carrots are cooking, spread almonds in single layer in 8- or 10-inch skillet; cook and stir over medium-high heat 4 to 7 minutes or until lightly browned.

3 Drain carrots; return to saucepan. Stir in marmalade and raisins. Cook over low heat about 1 minute, stirring constantly, until marmalade is melted. Add almonds; toss gently.

1 Serving: Calories 150 (Calories from Fat 20); Fat 2g (Saturated 0g); Cholesterol 0mg; Sodium 35mg; Carbohydrate 31g (Dietary Fiber 4g); Protein 2g. **Diet Exchanges:** 3 Vegetable, 1 Fruit, 1/2 Fat.

Betty's Simple Substitution

Marmalade and raisin lovers will love this easy, sweet glaze. Try it with other cooked vegetables; it does wonders for green beans, pea pods and broccoli.

Cheese Grits

Prep: 20 min   **Bake:** 40 min   **Stand:** 10 min   **8 servings**

2 cups milk

2 cups water

1/2 teaspoon salt

1/4 teaspoon pepper

1 cup uncooked white
hominy quick grits

1 1/2 cups shredded
Cheddar cheese (6 ounces)

2 medium green onions,
sliced (2 tablespoons)

2 eggs, slightly beaten

1 tablespoon butter
or margarine

1/4 teaspoon paprika

1 Heat oven to 350°. Spray bottom and sides of 1 1/2-quart casserole with cooking spray.

2 Heat milk, water, salt and pepper to boiling in 2-quart saucepan. Gradually add grits, stirring constantly; reduce heat to low. Simmer uncovered about 5 minutes, stirring frequently, until thickened. Stir in cheese and onions.

3 Stir 1 cup of the grits mixture into eggs, then stir back into remaining grits in saucepan. Pour into casserole. Cut butter into small pieces; sprinkle over grits. Sprinkle with paprika.

4 Bake uncovered 35 to 40 minutes or until set. Let stand 10 minutes before serving.

1 Serving: Calories 220 (Calories from Fat 100); Fat 11g (Saturated 7g); Cholesterol 85mg; Sodium 620mg; Carbohydrate 19g (Dietary Fiber 0g); Protein 11g. **Diet Exchanges:** 1 Starch, 1 Medium-Fat Meat, 1 Fat.

Bacon and Garlic Cheese Grits: Add 4 cloves garlic, peeled and finely chopped, with the cheese and onions and sprinkle cooked bacon bits over the grits just before serving.

Betty's
Special Touch

If you want an extra flavor boost, add a dash of cayenne pepper or red pepper flakes, or serve with salsa.

Slow Cooker Wild Rice with Cranberries

Prep: 15 min   **Cook:** 5 hr 15 min   **6 servings**

1 1/2 cups uncooked wild rice

1 tablespoon butter or margarine, melted

1/2 teaspoon salt

1/4 teaspoon pepper

4 medium green onions, sliced (1/4 cup)

2 cans (14 ounces each) vegetable broth

1 can (4 ounces) sliced mushrooms, undrained

1/2 cup slivered almonds

1/3 cup dried cranberries or dried cherries

1 Mix all ingredients except almonds and cranberries in 2- to 3 1/2-quart slow cooker.

2 Cover and cook on low heat setting 4 to 5 hours or until wild rice is tender.

3 Meanwhile, cook almonds in ungreased heavy skillet over medium-low heat 5 to 7 minutes, stirring frequently until browning begins, then stirring constantly until golden brown; set aside.

4 Stir almonds and cranberries into rice mixture. Cover and cook on low heat setting 15 minutes.

1 Serving: Calories 280 (Calories from Fat 65); Fat 7g (Saturated 2g); Cholesterol 5mg; Sodium 970mg; Carbohydrate 45g (Dietary Fiber 5g); Protein 9g. **Diet Exchanges:** 3 Starch, 1/2 Fat.

Betty's Special Touch

Here's a great way to cook your wild rice—in the slow cooker! Toasting the almonds not only enhances the flavor and color of the almonds, but also helps prevent them from becoming soggy after they're stirred into the wild rice mixture.

More Great Main Dishes

Delicious Drinks

Savor a welcoming cup of warm cider before the feast. Raise a toast to the season with a cold glass of punch. Relax after dinner with one of these satisfying sippers. Or serve wine with the meal—pairing wine with food is all about flavor and weight. The wine should complement the food and not overpower it, and vice versa.

Simple Sippers

- **Hot Spiced Cider:** Heat 10 cups apple cider, 1 teaspoon whole cloves, 1/2 teaspoon ground nutmeg and 6 sticks cinnamon to boiling in large saucepan over medium-high heat; reduce heat and simmer 10 minutes. Strain to remove whole spices. Keep hot in slow cooker. 10 servings.

- **Cinnamon-Orange Cider:** Heat 1/2 bottle (64-ounce size) apple cider (4 cups), 2 cups orange juice, 2 tablespoons red cinnamon candies and 1 1/2 teaspoons whole allspice to boiling in large saucepan; reduce heat. Cover and simmer 5 minutes. Strain to remove allspice. Stir in 1 tablespoon honey. Serve warm. 8 servings.

- **Cranberry Spice Tea:** Heat 3 cups brewed tea, 3 cups cranberry juice cocktail, 2 tablespoons sugar and 3 sticks cinnamon to boiling in large saucepan; reduce heat. Simmer uncovered 20 minutes, stirring occasionally. Remove cinnamon sticks. Serve warm. 6 servings.

- **Mint Iced Tea:** Combine 8 cups cold water, 1 cup packed fresh mint leaves and 6 tea bags in 2-quart pitcher. Stir to bruise mint leaves. Refrigerate overnight. Remove tea bags and mint leaves. Serve in tall glasses with ice. Serve with sugar, if desired. 8 servings.

- **Sparkling Cranberry Punch:** Mix 1 can (12 ounces) frozen lemonade concentrate, thawed, and 1 1/2 cups cold water in pitcher. Stir in 1 bottle (64 ounces) cranberry juice cocktail, chilled. Pour into punch bowl. Just before serving, stir in 4 cans (12 ounces each) ginger ale, chilled. Add ice cubes. Garnish with sliced strips of orange, lemon or lime peel and mint leaves. 24 servings.

- **Super-Easy Raspberry Punch:** Cook 4 packages (10 ounces each) frozen raspberries, thawed and undrained, in 4-quart Dutch oven over medium heat 10 minutes, stirring frequently; cool slightly. Push through strainer with large spoon to remove seeds. Refrigerate raspberry juice at least 2 hours. Mix raspberry juice and 1 can (6 ounces) frozen lemonade concentrate, thawed, in punch bowl or large pitcher. Stir in 1 bottle (2 liters) ginger ale, chilled. Serve immediately over ice. 24 servings.

Winning Wine Tips

- **Turkey** is probably the centerpiece of your meal, and very versatile, so many different styles of wine work well. If you prefer white wine, Gewürztraminer or Chardonnay are good choices. If you prefer red wine, try Pinot Noir.
- **Lighter foods** such as grilled fish and chicken, marry well with a light white wine with some acidity, such as Sauvignon Blanc or some Chardonnays.
- **Hearty foods** such as beef need a heavier red wine that is bold enough to stand up to the food, such as Cabernet Sauvignon or Shiraz.
- **Sweet foods and dishes with some sweetness** such as fruit-based sauces are best paired with a white wine that also has a touch of sweetness, such as Riesling.
- **Sour foods** made with lemons, limes and vinegar cut the tartness of a wine and make a full-bodied wine taste sweet and thin. Instead, choose a white wine that also has some acidity, such as Sauvignon Blanc.
- **Spicy, smoked and heavily seasoned foods** are best served with light, fruity wines such as Pinot Noir (red) or Sauvignon Blanc (white) that tend to cool the heat.

Food and Wine Pairings

There is no single perfect wine for any one food. If you like a wine, drink it with food you like, and you're sure to have a super match.

Food	Wine
Beef	Cabernet, Shiraz/Syrah
Chicken	Chardonnay
Desserts	Champagne, Riesling, Port
Fish and Shellfish	Chardonnay, Sauvignon Blanc
Ham	Shiraz, Riesling
Pasta	Merlot, Zinfandel
Pork	Cabernet, Zinfandel
Turkey	Gewürztraminer, Chardonnay, Pinot Noir

Sweet and Spicy Rubbed Ham

Prep: 10 min   **Bake:** 1 hr 30 min   **Stand:** 15 min   **18 servings**

6- to 8-pound fully cooked smoked bone-in ham

1/2 cup packed brown sugar

1/3 cup maple-flavored syrup

1/2 teaspoon ground mustard

1/8 teaspoon ground cinnamon

1/8 teaspoon ground ginger

1/8 teaspoon ground cloves

Dash of ground nutmeg

1 Heat oven to 325°. Line shallow roasting pan with aluminum foil. Place ham, cut side down, on rack in pan. Insert meat thermometer so tip is in center of thickest part of ham and does not touch bone. Bake uncovered about 1 hour 30 minutes or until thermometer reads 135° to 140°.

2 While ham is baking, mix remaining ingredients. Brush over ham during last 30 minutes of baking.

3 Cover ham loosely with tent of aluminum foil. Let stand 10 to 15 minutes for easiest carving.

1 Serving: Calories 130 (Calories from Fat 35); Fat 4g (Saturated 1g); Cholesterol 35mg; Sodium 880mg; Carbohydrate 9g (Dietary Fiber 0g); Protein 15g. **Diet Exchanges:** 2 Very Lean Meat, 1/2 Fruit.

Betty's Special Touch

Try either Apple-Cranberry Chutney (page 64) or Tangy Cherry Sauce (page 62) as an excellent accompaniment to this flavorful ham. Garnish with red grapes, watercress and cinnamon sticks for an easy yet impressive look.

Heartland Favorites

Serves 15

Farming still retains much of its original character in the Midwest and nation's interior, from North Dakota to northern Texas. Hearty, straightforward cooking styles are the norm here, with Scandinavian and German influences in many parts of this region.

So-Simple Cranberry Gelatin Salad, page 137
Sweet and Spicy Rubbed Ham, above
Cranberry-Apple Glazed Turkey, page 19
Classic Pan Gravy, page 48
Classic Bread Stuffing or Sausage Stuffing, page 52
Classic Green Bean Casserole, page 69
Classic Sweet Potatoes with Marshmallows, page 75
Do-Ahead Dinner Rolls, page 112
Impossibly Easy Pumpkin Pie, page 157
Apple Pudding Cake with Cinnamon Butter Sauce, page 169

Baked Ham with Zesty Cranberry Sauce

Prep: 20 min   **Bake:** 2 hr   **Stand:** 15 min   **18 servings**

6- to 8-pound fully cooked smoked bone-in ham

1 can (16 ounces) jellied cranberry sauce

1/3 cup apple juice

1/4 cup port wine

2 tablespoons lemon juice

1 tablespoon Dijon mustard

2 teaspoons sugar

2 teaspoons grated lemon peel

2 teaspoons grated orange peel

1/4 teaspoon white pepper

1/4 teaspoon ground ginger

1 Heat oven to 325°. Place ham, cut side down, on rack in shallow roasting pan. Pour water into pan until 1/4 to 1/2 inch deep. Insert meat thermometer so tip is in center of thickest part of ham and does not touch bone.

2 Cover with aluminum foil. Bake 1 hour 30 minutes to 2 hours, uncovering ham after 45 minutes, until meat thermometer reads 135° to 140°. Let stand 10 to 15 minutes for easiest carving.

3 While ham is baking, beat remaining ingredients in 1-quart saucepan with wire whisk until well mixed. Cook over medium heat about 10 minutes, stirring frequently, until cranberry sauce is melted and mixture is hot. Serve sauce with sliced ham.

1 Serving: Calories 165 (Calories from Fat 45); Fat 5g (Saturated 1g); Cholesterol 45mg; Sodium 1010mg; Carbohydrate 13g (Dietary Fiber 0g); Protein 17g. **Diet Exchanges:** 2 1/2 Very Lean Meat, 1 Fruit, 1/2 Fat.

Betty's Do-Ahead

The Zesty Cranberry Sauce can be cooked 2 to 3 days ahead of time and stored covered in the refrigerator. About 5 to 10 minutes before serving, heat sauce to serve with ham.

Pork Crown Roast
with Cranberry Stuffing

Prep: 20 min   **Bake:** 3 hr 20 min   **Stand:** 20 min   **15 servings**

(see photo insert)

7 1/2- to 8-pound pork crown roast (about 14 to 16 ribs)

2 teaspoons salt

1 teaspoon pepper

Cranberry Stuffing (page 57)

1 Heat oven to 325°. Sprinkle pork with salt and pepper. Place pork, bone ends up, on rack in shallow roasting pan. Wrap bone ends in aluminum foil to prevent excessive browning. Insert meat thermometer so tip is in center of thickest part of meat and does not touch bone or rest in fat. Place small heatproof bowl or crumpled aluminum foil in crown to hold shape of roast evenly.

2 Bake uncovered 2 hours 30 minutes to 3 hours 20 minutes or until thermometer reads 155°.

3 While pork is baking, make Cranberry Stuffing. One hour before pork is done, remove bowl and fill center of crown with stuffing. Cover only stuffing with aluminum foil for first 30 minutes. Remove pork from oven, cover with tent of aluminum foil. Let stand 15 to 20 minutes or until thermometer reads 160°. (Temperature will continue to rise about 5°, and pork will be easier to carve.)

4 Remove foil wrapping; place paper frills on bone ends if desired. To serve, spoon stuffing into bowl and cut pork between ribs.

1 Serving: Calories 415 (Calories from Fat 215); Fat 24g (Saturated 12g); Cholesterol 120mg; Sodium 830mg; Carbohydrate 17g (Dietary Fiber 1g); Protein 33g. **Diet Exchanges:** 1 Starch, 4 Medium-Fat Meat, 1 Fat.

Betty's Do-Ahead

This special roast may be on hand at your supermarket during the holidays, but call the meat department ahead of time to make sure. The fancy paper frills usually come with the roast.

Grilled Pork and Apples with Red Onion Chutney

Prep: 45 min   **Grill:** 22 min

6 servings

1 tablespoon vegetable oil

1 1/2 cups chopped red onion

1/2 cup packed brown sugar

1/3 cup red wine vinegar

1/4 cup diced dried fruit and raisin mixture

1/4 teaspoon pumpkin pie spice

2 pork tenderloins (3/4 pound each)

3 apples, cored and cut crosswise into 1/2-inch rings

1 Heat oil in 2-quart saucepan over medium heat. Cook onion in oil about 8 minutes, stirring frequently, until onion is tender. Mix 2 tablespoons of the brown sugar and 4 teaspoons of the vinegar in small bowl; reserve.

2 Stir remaining brown sugar and vinegar, the dried fruits and pumpkin pie spice into onion. Heat to boiling; reduce heat to low. Cook 20 to 25 minutes or until dried fruits are plump and mixture has thickened; remove from heat.

3 Heat coals or gas grill for direct heat. Lightly brush some of the reserved brown sugar mixture over pork. Place pork on grill rack 4 to 6 inches from medium heat. Cover and grill 18 to 22 minutes, turning once, until pork is slightly pink in center.

4 Lightly brush apple rings with remaining brown sugar mixture. Place apple rings on grill for last 10 minutes of grilling. Cut pork diagonally into slices. Serve with grilled apples and chutney.

1 Serving: Calories 310 (Calories from Fat 65); Fat 7g (Saturated 2g); Cholesterol 70mg; Sodium 60mg; Carbohydrate 36g (Dietary Fiber 3g); Protein 26g. **Diet Exchanges:** 4 Very Lean Meat, 2 1/2 Fruit.

Betty's Simple Substitution

If you'd like to make this special pork dish but don't have a grill, you can broil it. Place pork on broiler pan; broil 4 to 6 inches from heat using times above as a guide, turning pork once and placing apple rings on pan during last 10 minutes of broiling time. Serve with the chutney.

Marinated Beef Tenderloin with Merlot Sauce

Prep: 10 min   **Marinate:** 8 hr   **Roast:** 45 min   **Stand:** 20 min   **12 servings**

(see photo insert)

3-pound beef tenderloin

1/3 cup red wine vinegar

1/3 cup olive or vegetable oil

2 tablespoons chopped fresh or 2 teaspoons dried basil leaves

2 tablespoons chopped fresh or 2 teaspoons dried oregano leaves

2 tablespoons chopped fresh parsley or 2 teaspoons parsley flakes

1/2 teaspoon freshly ground pepper

2 cloves garlic, finely chopped

Merlot Sauce (below)

1 Place beef in resealable plastic food-storage bag or large glass or plastic dish. Mix remaining ingredients except Merlot Sauce; pour over beef. Seal bag or cover dish and refrigerate at least 8 hours but no longer than 24 hours, turning beef several times to coat with marinade.

2 Heat oven to 425°. Remove beef from marinade; discard marinade. Place beef on rack in shallow roasting pan. Insert meat thermometer so tip is in center of thickest part of beef.

3 Roast uncovered 40 to 45 minutes or until thermometer reads 140° (medium-rare doneness). Cover beef loosely with tent of aluminum foil. Let stand 15 to 20 minutes or until thermometer reads 145°. (Temperature will continue to rise about 5° and beef will be easier to carve as juices set up.)

4 While beef is standing, make Merlot Sauce. Cut beef across grain at slanted angle into thin slices. Serve with sauce.

1 Serving: Calories 290 (Calories from Fat 115); Fat 13g (Saturated 5g); Cholesterol 70mg; Sodium 120mg; Carbohydrate 18g (Dietary Fiber 0g); Protein 25g. **Diet Exchanges:** 3 1/2 Lean Meat, 1 Fruit, 1 Fat.

Merlot Sauce

1 cup currant jelly

1 cup Merlot, Zinfandel or nonalcoholic red wine

1/2 cup beef broth

2 tablespoons butter or margarine

Heat all ingredients to boiling in 1-quart saucepan, stirring occasionally; reduce heat to low. Simmer uncovered 10 to 15 minutes, stirring occasionally, until sauce is slightly reduced and syrupy.

Betty's Do-Ahead

Get a jump on preparing this tasty main dish the day ahead by marinating the beef the evening before the big day. The sauce can be made up to 3 days in advance and stored covered in the refrigerator. About 5 to 10 minutes before serving, heat the sauce and serve with the beef.

Cranberry-Wine Venison Steaks

Prep: 20 min   **Marinate:** 2 hr   **Cook:** 15 min   **4 servings**

1/2 cup dry red wine or nonalcoholic red wine

1 tablespoon Dijon mustard

4 venison tenderloin steaks, about 1 inch thick (1 1/4 pounds)

1/4 teaspoon salt

1/4 teaspoon coarsely ground pepper

1 tablespoon olive or vegetable oil

1/2 cup beef broth

1/2 cup dried cranberries

2 tablespoons currant or apple jelly

1 tablespoon butter or margarine

2 medium green onions, sliced (2 tablespoons)

1 Mix wine and mustard until well blended. Place venison in resealable plastic food-storage bag or shallow glass or plastic dish. Pour wine mixture over venison; turn venison to coat with marinade. Seal bag or cover dish and refrigerate at least 2 hours but no longer than 4 hours, turning venison occasionally.

2 Remove venison from marinade; reserve marinade. Sprinkle venison with salt and pepper. Heat oil in 12-inch nonstick skillet over medium-high heat. Cook venison in oil about 4 minutes, turning once, until brown.

3 Add broth to skillet; reduce heat to low. Cover and cook about 10 minutes, turning venison once, until venison is tender and desired doneness. (Don't overcook or venison will become tough.)

4 Remove venison from skillet; keep warm. Stir marinade into skillet. Heat to boiling, scraping up any bits from bottom of skillet; reduce heat to medium. Cook about 5 minutes or until mixture is slightly reduced. Stir in cranberries, jelly, butter and onions. Cook 1 to 2 minutes, stirring occasionally, until butter is melted and mixture is hot. Serve sauce with venison.

1 Serving: Calories 300 (Calories from Fat 90); Fat 10g (Saturated 4g); Cholesterol 125mg; Sodium 450mg; Carbohydrate 20g (Dietary Fiber 1g), Protein 33g. **Diet Exchanges:** 4 1/2 Lean Meat, 1 Fruit.

Betty's Do-Ahead

Did you know the Pilgrims served venison at the first Thanksgiving? The wine and mustard serve as a marinade to tenderize the venison, and it also helps you start your meal ahead of time. Because this step is done 2 to 4 hours before cooking, you can work on other preparation while the meat is marinating.

Garlic- and Rosemary-Marinated Leg of Lamb with Apricot Sauce

Prep: 20 min   **Marinate:** 8 hr   **Bake:** 2 hr   **Stand:** 15 min   **8 servings**

5-pound bone-in leg of lamb

8 small cloves garlic, cut lengthwise in half

4 rosemary sprigs, each about 4 inches long, cut into 4 pieces

1 can (15 to 16 ounces) apricot halves in light syrup, drained and syrup reserved

1/2 cup dry red wine or nonalcoholic red wine

1/4 cup olive or vegetable oil

2 tablespoons honey

1/4 teaspoon salt

1 teaspoon chopped fresh rosemary leaves

1 Make 16 small slits, each about 1/2 inch wide and 1 inch deep, over surface of lamb. Insert 1 garlic and 1 rosemary piece in each slit using tip of knife. Place lamb in large resealable plastic food-storage bag or shallow glass or plastic dish.

2 Mix reserved apricot syrup, the wine, oil, 1 tablespoon of the honey and the salt; pour over lamb. Seal bag or cover dish and refrigerate at least 8 hours but no longer than 24 hours, turning lamb occasionally.

3 Heat oven to 325°. Remove lamb from marinade; reserve marinade. Place lamb, fat side up, on rack in shallow roasting pan. Insert meat thermometer so tip is in thickest part of lamb and does not touch bone or rest in fat.

4 Bake uncovered about 2 hours, brushing once or twice with marinade, until thermometer reads 140°. Cover lamb loosely with tent of aluminum foil. Let stand 10 to 15 minutes or until thermometer reads 145°. (Temperature will continue to rise about 5 degrees, and lamb will be easier to carve.) Reserve 1/4 cup marinade; discard any remaining marinade.

5 While lamb is standing, place apricots in food processor or blender. Cover and process until smooth. Mix apricots, 1/4 cup marinade, remaining 1 tablespoon honey and the chopped rosemary in 1-quart saucepan. Heat to boiling. Boil 1 to 2 minutes, stirring occasionally. Serve sauce with lamb. Garnish with additional apricot halves and fresh rosemary leaves if desired.

1 Serving: Calories 395 (Calories from Fat 160); Fat 18g (Saturated 5g); Cholesterol 125mg; Sodium 170mg; Carbohydrate 18g (Dietary Fiber 1g); Protein 40g. **Diet Exchanges:** 6 Lean Meat, 1 Fruit.

Betty's Special Touch

To serve, place this special lamb dish on a platter lined with fresh rosemary sprigs and apricot halves.

Roast Goose
with Apple Stuffing

Prep: 1 hr 30 min   **Roast:** 3 hr 30 min   **Stand:** 15 min   **Cook:** 10 min   **16 servings**

8- to 10-pound goose, thawed if frozen

2 cups water

1 small onion, sliced

3/4 teaspoon salt

6 cups soft bread crumbs (about 9 slices bread)

1/4 cup butter or margarine, melted

1 1/2 teaspoons chopped fresh or 1/2 teaspoon dried sage leaves

3/4 teaspoon chopped fresh or 1/4 teaspoon dried thyme leaves

1/2 teaspoon salt

1/4 teaspoon pepper

3 medium tart apples, chopped (3 cups)

2 medium stalks celery (with leaves), chopped (1 cup)

1 medium onion, chopped (1/2 cup)

1/4 cup all-purpose flour

1 Prepare goose for roasting as directed for turkey (page 15). Remove excess fat from goose.

2 Heat giblets and neck, water, sliced onion and 3/4 teaspoon salt to boiling in 1-quart saucepan; reduce heat. Cover and simmer about 1 hour or until giblets are tender. Strain broth; cover and refrigerate. Remove meat from neck and finely chop with giblets and onion. Toss giblets and remaining ingredients except flour in large bowl.

3 Heat oven to 350°. Fill neck cavity lightly with apple stuffing. Fasten neck skin to back of goose with skewer. Fold wings across back of goose so tips are touching. Fill body cavity lightly with stuffing. (Do not pack stuffing because it will expand during roasting.) Tuck drumsticks under band of skin at tail, or tie together with heavy string, then tie to tail. Pierce skin all over with fork.

4 Place goose, breast side up, on rack in deep roasting pan. Insert oven-proof meat thermometer so tip is in thickest part of inside thigh muscle and does not touch bone. (Do not add water or cover goose.)

5 Roast uncovered 3 hours to 3 hours 30 minutes, removing excess fat from pan occasionally with a heatproof bulb baster or a large spoon. After roasting about 2 hours, place a tent of aluminum foil loosely over goose when it begins to turn golden, and cut band of skin or remove tie holding drumsticks to allow inside of thighs to cook through.

6 Goose is done when thermometer reads 180° and juices are no longer pink when center of thigh is cut. Thermometer placed in center of stuffing will read 165°. If a meat thermometer is not used, begin testing for doneness after 2 hours 30 minutes. When goose is done, place on warm platter and cover with aluminum foil. Let stand about 15 minutes for easiest carving.

7 Pour drippings from pan into bowl; skim off fat. Return 1/4 cup drippings to pan (discard remaining drippings). Stir in flour. Cook over medium heat, stirring constantly, until smooth and bubbly; remove from heat.

8 Add enough water to reserved giblet broth, if necessary, to measure 2 cups. Stir into flour mixture. Heat to boiling, stirring constantly. Boil and stir 1 minute. Serve goose with apple stuffing and gravy. Cover and refrigerate any remaining goose and stuffing separately.

Betty's Helpful Tip

For easy cleanup, line the roasting pan with aluminum foil before placing the goose on the rack in the roasting pan.

1 Serving: Calories 415 (Calories from Fat 245); Fat 27g (Saturated 9g); Cholesterol 105mg; Sodium 400mg; Carbohydrate 14g (Dietary Fiber 1g); Protein 29g. **Diet Exchanges:** 4 Medium-Fat Meat, 1 Fruit, 1 Fat.

Pheasant with Oregano Cream Sauce

Prep: 30 min   **Cook:** 10 min   **Bake:** 1 hr 30 min   **6 servings**

2 pheasants (2 1/2 to 3 pounds each), thawed if frozen

1/2 cup all-purpose flour

1/2 teaspoon seasoned salt

1/4 teaspoon pepper

2 tablespoons vegetable oil

1 package (8 ounces) whole mushrooms

2 cups baby-cut carrots

1 tablespoon butter or margarine

1 cup half-and-half

1/2 cup chicken broth

2 tablespoons dry sherry or chicken broth

1 tablespoon chopped fresh or 1/2 teaspoon dried oregano leaves

1 Heat oven to 350°. Cut each pheasant in half along backbone and breastbone from tail to neck with kitchen scissors. Mix flour, seasoned salt and pepper in shallow bowl. Coat pheasant generously with flour mixture. Reserve remaining flour mixture.

2 Heat oil in 12-inch skillet over medium-high heat. Cook pheasants in oil 3 to 4 minutes on each side or until well browned. Place in ungreased rectangular pan, 13 × 9 × 2 inches, or in shallow roasting pan. Top and surround pheasants with mushrooms and carrots.

3 Melt butter in 2-quart saucepan over medium heat. Add enough additional flour to remaining flour mixture to make 2 tablespoons. Stir flour mixture into butter. Cook, stirring constantly, until mixture is smooth and bubbly; remove from heat. Gradually stir in half-and-half and broth. Heat to boiling, stirring constantly. Boil and stir 1 minute. Stir in sherry and oregano. Pour evenly over pheasants.

4 Bake uncovered 1 hour 15 minutes to 1 hour 30 minutes, spooning sauce in pan over pheasants once, until pheasants are tender and juice is no longer pink when centers of thickest pieces are cut. Remove pheasants from pan with slotted spoon. Stir sauce until smooth. Serve sauce with pheasants.

1 Serving: Calories 740 (Calories from Fat 360); Fat 40g (Saturated 14g); Cholesterol 230mg; Sodium 500mg; Carbohydrate 18g (Dietary Fiber 2g); Protein 76g. **Diet Exchanges:** 1/2 Starch, 6 Lean Meat.

Betty's Simple Substitution

Back from hunting empty-handed? You can use chicken instead of pheasant in this dish. If you don't have oregano, either fresh or dried rosemary or thyme would be great substitutes in this flavorful pheasant dish.

Sage-Garlic Roast Chicken

Prep: 15 min   **Roast:** 1 hr 30 min   **Stand:** 15 min   **6 servings**

3 1/2- to 4-pound whole broiler-fryer chicken, thawed if frozen

2 tablespoons chopped fresh sage leaves

1 tablespoon chopped fresh parsley

1 teaspoon dried thyme leaves

3 cloves garlic, chopped

1 teaspoon vegetable oil

2 tablespoons butter or margarine, softened

1/2 teaspoon salt

1/8 teaspoon pepper

1 Heat oven to 375°. Prepare chicken for roasting as directed for turkey (page 15).

2 Mix sage, parsley, thyme and garlic until blended. Place 1 tablespoon of the herb mixture in small bowl; stir in oil and set aside.

3 Place chicken, breast side up, on rack in shallow roasting pan. Loosen breast and thigh skin gently with fingers as far back as possible. Rub remaining herb mixture under skin of chicken. Rub butter on outer skin. Sprinkle chicken with salt and pepper. Insert ovenproof meat thermometer so tip is in thickest part of inside thigh muscle and does not touch bone. (Do not add water or cover chicken.)

4 Roast uncovered 1 hour 15 minutes to 1 hour 30 minutes. During last 5 minutes of roasting, brush reserved herb-oil mixture over chicken.

5 Chicken is done when thermometer reads 180° and juice of chicken is no longer pink when you cut into center of thigh. If a meat thermometer is not used, begin testing for doneness after about 1 hour. When chicken is done, place on warm platter and cover with aluminum foil to keep warm. Let stand about 15 minutes for easiest carving.

1 Serving: Calories 310 (Calories from Fat 180); Fat 20g (Saturated 7g); Cholesterol 110mg; Sodium 230mg; Carbohydrate 1g (Dietary Fiber 0g); Protein 31g. **Diet Exchanges:** 4 1/2 Lean Meat, 1 1/2 Fat.

Betty's Special Touch

You can use any combination of fresh herbs in this recipe. A little bit of rosemary delivers lots of flavor. Center chicken on a decorative platter, and surround with Roasted Autumn Vegetables (page 82). Garnish with sprigs of sage and parsley.

Thanksgiving Together

Serves 2

If you normally cook for two, you know it can be quite a challenge to find recipes and foods geared to just two.

Citrus Fruit Salad, page 144
Sage-Garlic Roast Chicken, above
or Cornish Hen with Bulgur-Bacon Stuffing, page 104
No-Drippings Gravy, page 49
Apple-Cranberry Chutney, page 64
Bountiful Twice-Baked Potatoes (1/2 recipe), page 74
Easy Green Beans and Cranberries (1/2 recipe), page 70
Purchased Dinner Rolls or Oatmeal-Cranberry Muffins, page 118
Cranberry Mousse, page 177 or Chocolate Truffle Brownie Cups, page 179

Cornish Hen with Bulgur-Bacon Stuffing

Prep: 25 min   **Cook:** 15 min   **Bake:** 1 hr 15 min   **Stand:** 15 min   **2 servings**

Bulgur-Bacon Stuffing
(below)

1 1/2-pound Rock Cornish
hen, thawed if frozen

1 tablespoon butter
or margarine, melted

1 Make Bulgur-Bacon Stuffing.

2 Heat oven to 350°. Fill body cavity of hen with stuffing. Fasten opening with skewer. Place hen, breast side up, on rack in shallow roasting pan. Insert meat thermometer so tip is in thickest part of thigh muscle and does not touch bone. Brush with some of the butter.

3 Bake uncovered 1 hour to 1 hour 15 minutes, brushing occasionally with remaining butter, until thermometer reads 180° and juices are no longer pink when center of thigh is cut.

4 Remove stuffing from body cavity. Cut hen in half along backbone and breastbone from tail to neck with kitchen scissors. Serve each hen half with stuffing.

1 Serving: Calories 405 (Calories from Fat 245); Fat 27g (Saturated 9g); Cholesterol 165mg; Sodium 790mg; Carbohydrate 15g (Dietary Fiber 3g); Protein 29g. **Diet Exchanges:** 1 Starch, 4 Lean Meat, 2 Fat.

Bulgur-Bacon Stuffing

1 slice bacon, chopped

1 small onion, chopped
(1/4 cup)

1/4 cup water

1 teaspoon chicken
bouillon granules

3 tablespoons uncooked
bulgur

1/4 cup shredded
zucchini

1/4 cup chopped fresh
mushrooms

1/2 teaspoon chopped
fresh or 1/8 teaspoon
dried thyme leaves

Cook bacon and onion in 1-quart saucepan over medium-high heat, stirring frequently, until bacon is cooked and onion is tender; drain bacon drippings. Remove bacon and onion from pan; set aside. Heat water and bouillon granules to boiling in same saucepan. Stir in bulgur; remove from heat. Cover and let stand 15 minutes. Stir in bacon mixture, zucchini, mushrooms and thyme.

Betty's Simple Substitution

With a mild flavor and chewy texture, bulgur is a great stand-in for rice in nearly any recipe. No chicken bouillon granules on hand? Omit the 1/4 cup water and use 1/4 cup chicken broth instead.

Salmon with Cranberry-Pistachio Sauce

Prep: 10 min　　**Cook:** 20 min　　**Broil:** 10 min　　　　　　　　**8 servings**

Cranberry-Pistachio
Sauce (below)

2-pound salmon fillet

**2 tablespoons fresh lime
juice**

**2 tablespoons butter
or margarine, melted**

1/2 teaspoon salt

**Chopped pistachio nuts,
if desired**

1 Make Cranberry-Pistachio Sauce; keep warm.

2 Set oven control to broil. Spray broiler pan rack with cooking spray. Place salmon, skin side down, on rack in broiler pan. Mix lime juice, butter and salt; pour over salmon.

3 Broil with top 4 inches from heat 8 to 10 minutes or until salmon flakes easily with fork. Top with sauce. Sprinkle with nuts.

1 Serving: Calories 485 (Calories from Fat 110); Fat 12g (Saturated 4g); Cholesterol 80mg; Sodium 220mg; Carbohydrate 68g (Dietary Fiber 4g); Protein 26g. **Diet Exchanges:** 4 Lean Meat, 4 1/2 Fruit.

Cranberry-Pistachio Sauce

**1 pound fresh or frozen
cranberries**

1 cup sugar

**1 jar (10 ounces)
red currant jelly**

1 cup orange juice

**1/2 cup chopped
pistachio nuts**

Mix cranberries, sugar, jelly and orange juice in 2-quart saucepan. Heat to boiling; reduce heat. Simmer uncovered 20 minutes, skimming off any foam that collects on surface; remove from heat. Stir in nuts.

Betty's Do-Ahead

You can make this Cranberry-Pistachio Sauce up to 1 week ahead of time; keep covered in the refrigerator. The sauce also makes a great hostess gift—just fill a decorative jar or container.

Deviled Lobster Tails

Prep: 45 min   **Bake:** 10 min

4 servings

2 teaspoons salt

4 frozen lobster tails
(about 10 ounces each)

2 tablespoons butter
or margarine

4 medium green onions,
sliced (1/4 cup)

2 tablespoons all-purpose
flour

1 1/2 cups half-and-half

1/4 cup cocktail sauce

2 teaspoons
Worcestershire sauce

1 teaspoon ground
mustard

1/2 teaspoon salt

1/2 teaspoon red pepper
sauce

2 tablespoons butter
or margarine, melted

1/3 cup dry bread
crumbs

1 Heat 2 quarts water and 2 teaspoons salt to boiling in 6-quart Dutch oven; add lobster tails. Heat to boiling; reduce heat to low. Cover and simmer 8 to 10 minutes or until lobster tails turn bright red and meat is opaque. Immediately plunge lobster tails into cold water to stop cooking. (Lobster will not be thoroughly cooked but will continue to cook during baking step.)

2 Meanwhile, heat oven to 450°. Melt 2 tablespoons butter in 2-quart saucepan over medium heat. Cook onions in butter about 2 minutes, stirring occasionally, until onions are tender. Stir in flour; cook and stir until mixture is smooth and bubbly. Gradually stir in half-and-half, stirring constantly. Heat to boiling; cook 1 minute, stirring constantly. Stir in cocktail sauce, Worcestershire sauce, mustard, 1/2 teaspoon salt and the pepper sauce until blended; remove from heat.

3 Cut and remove membrane from under side of each lobster tail, using kitchen scissors; discard membrane. Remove lobster meat from shells; reserve shells. Cut lobster into chunks; stir lobster into sauce until blended. Fill reserved shells with lobster mixture. Place shells in ungreased shallow baking dish. (If necessary, place crumpled aluminum foil between lobster tails to prevent shells from tipping.)

4 Mix 2 tablespoons melted butter and the bread crumbs until blended. Sprinkle over lobster mixture. Bake uncovered about 10 minutes or until heated through and bread crumbs are browned.

1 Serving: Calories 360 (Calories from Fat 210); Fat 23g (Saturated 14g); Cholesterol 110mg; Sodium 1280mg; Carbohydrate 20g (Dietary Fiber 1g); Protein 18g. **Diet Exchanges:** 1 Starch, 2 Lean Meat, 4 Fat.

Betty's Helpful Tip

Frozen lobster tails weigh between 8 and 12 ounces each, and cooking time depends on the size of the tails. Cocktail sauces have variable levels of heat, so choose a sauce according to your heat preference.

Roasted-Vegetable Lasagna

Prep: 30 min   **Bake:** 50 min   **Cook:** 25 min   **Stand:** 10 min   **10 servings**

Olive oil-flavored
cooking spray

2 medium bell peppers,
cut into 1-inch pieces

1 medium onion, cut into
8 wedges and separated
into pieces

2 medium zucchini, sliced
(4 cups)

8 ounces mushrooms,
sliced (3 cups)

Cooking spray

1/2 teaspoon salt

1/4 teaspoon pepper

Tomato Sauce (below)

12 uncooked lasagna
noodles

4 cups shredded mozzarella
cheese (16 ounces)

1 cup freshly grated
Parmesan cheese
(4 ounces)

1 Heat oven to 450°. Spray jelly roll pan, 15 1/2 × 10 1/2 × 1 inch, with cooking spray. Place bell peppers, onion, zucchini and mushrooms in single layer in pan. Spray vegetables with cooking spray; sprinkle with salt and pepper. Bake uncovered 20 to 25 minutes, turning vegetables once, until vegetables are tender.

2 While vegetables are baking, make Tomato Sauce.

3 Cook and drain noodles as directed on package. Rinse noodles with cold water; drain. Mix cheeses; set aside.

4 Reduce oven temperature to 400°. Spray rectangular baking dish, 13 1/2 × 9 × 2 inches, with cooking spray. Spread 1/4 cup of the Tomato Sauce in dish; top with 3 noodles. Layer with 3/4 cup sauce, 1 1/4 cups vegetables and 1 cup cheese. Repeat layering with remaining noodles, sauce, vegetables and cheese 3 more times.

5 Bake uncovered 20 to 25 minutes or until hot. Let stand 10 minutes before cutting.

1 Serving: Calories 320 (Calories from Fat 110); Fat 12g (Saturated 7g); Cholesterol 30mg; Sodium 780mg; Carbohydrate 31g (Dietary Fiber 3g); Protein 22g. **Diet Exchanges:** 2 Starch, 2 Medium-Fat Meat.

Tomato Sauce

1 large onion, chopped
(1 cup)

2 tablespoons finely
chopped garlic

1 can (28 ounces) crushed
tomatoes, undrained

3 tablespoons chopped
fresh or 1 tablespoon
dried basil leaves

3 tablespoons chopped
fresh or 1 tablespoon
dried oregano leaves

1 teaspoon sugar

1/2 teaspoon salt

1/2 teaspoon crushed
red pepper

Spray 2-quart saucepan with cooking spray. Cook onion and garlic in saucepan over medium heat 2 minutes, stirring occasionally. Stir in remaining ingredients. Heat to boiling; reduce heat. Simmer uncovered 15 to 20 minutes or until slightly thickened.

Betty's Do-Ahead

You can prepare the sauce the day before, or use 4 cups of prepared spaghetti sauce instead of the homemade tomato sauce. The entire lasagna can also be prepared the day before. Cover unbaked lasagna tightly with aluminum foil and refrigerate no longer than 24 hours. About 45 minutes before serving, heat oven to 400°. Uncover and bake 25 to 35 minutes or until hot.

Breads *and* Rolls

Home-Baked Rolls

There's nothing like fresh-baked rolls, warm from the oven. Add to the festivities at Thanksgiving by shaping your dinner rolls. These shapes are super-easy and delicious. As an added bonus, you can make the rolls ahead of time and freeze up to 2 months. Follow the Classic Dinner Rolls recipe (page 112), or use purchased frozen (thawed) bread dough.

Bow Knot Rolls

Lightly grease cookie sheets with shortening. After pushing fist into dough to deflate, divide half of the dough into 16 equal pieces. (To divide, cut dough in half, then continue cutting pieces in half until there are 16 pieces.) Roll each piece into 9-inch rope on lightly floured surface. Tie each into a loose knot. Place 2 to 3 inches apart on cookie sheet. Cover loosely with plastic wrap and let rise in warm place about 30 minutes or until double. Bake 12 to 15 minutes or until golden brown. Repeat with remaining dough. 32 rolls.

Cloverleaf Rolls

Grease bottoms and sides of 24 medium muffin cups, 2 1/2 × 1 1/4 inches, with shortening. After pushing fist into dough to deflate, divide dough into 72 equal pieces. (To divide, cut dough in half, then continue cutting pieces in half until there are 72 pieces.) Shape each piece into a ball. Place 3 balls in each muffin cup. Brush with butter. Cover loosely with plastic wrap and let rise in warm place about 30 minutes or until double. Bake as directed for Classic Dinner Rolls. 24 rolls.

Crescent Rolls

Grease cookie sheet with shortening. After pushing fist into dough to deflate, cut dough in half. Roll each half into 12 inch circle on floured surface. Spread with softened butter. Cut each circle into 16 wedges. Roll up each wedge, beginning at rounded edge. Place rolls, with points underneath, on cookie sheet and curve slightly. Brush with butter. Cover loosely with plastic wrap and let rise in warm place about 30 minutes or until double. Bake as directed for Classic Dinner Rolls. 32 rolls.

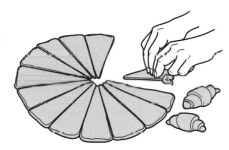

Crown Rolls

Lightly grease bottoms and sides of 12 medium muffin cups, 2 1/2 × 1 1/4 inches, with shortening. After pushing fist into dough to deflate, divide half of the dough into 12 equal pieces. (To divide, cut dough in half, then continue cutting pieces in half until there are 12 pieces.) Shape each piece into a ball, putting edges under to make a smooth top. Place 1 ball, smooth side up, in each muffin cup. Using kitchen scissors dipped in flour, cut balls of dough into fourths almost to bottom. Cover loosely with plastic wrap and let rise in warm place about 30 minutes or until double. Bake 14 to 18 minutes or until golden brown. Repeat with remaining dough. 24 rolls.

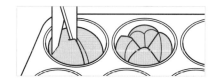

Classic Dinner Rolls

Prep: 30 min   **Rise:** 1 hr 30 min   **Bake:** 15 min   **15 rolls**

3 1/2 to 3 3/4 cups all-purpose flour or bread flour

1/4 cup sugar

1/4 cup butter or margarine, softened

1 teaspoon salt

1 package regular or quick active dry yeast (2 1/4 teaspoons)

1/2 cup very warm water (120° to 130°)

1/2 cup very warm milk (scalded* then cooled to 120° to 130°)

1 egg

Butter or margarine, melted, if desired

*To Scald Milk: Heat over medium heat until tiny bubbles form at the edge (do not boil).

1 Mix 2 cups of the flour, the sugar, 1/4 cup butter, salt and yeast in large bowl. Add warm water, warm milk and egg. Beat with electric mixer on low speed 1 minute, scraping bowl frequently. Beat on medium speed 1 minute, scraping bowl frequently. Stir in enough remaining flour to make dough easy to handle.

2 Place dough on lightly floured surface; gently roll in flour to coat. Knead about 5 minutes or until dough is smooth and springy. Place dough in large bowl greased with shortening, turning dough to grease all sides. Cover bowl loosely with plastic wrap and let rise in warm place about 1 hour or until double. Dough is ready if indentation remains when touched.

3 Grease bottom and sides of rectangular pan, 13 × 9 × 2 inches, with shortening. Gently push fist into dough to deflate. Divide dough into 15 equal pieces. Shape each piece into a ball; place in pan. Brush with melted butter. Cover loosely with plastic wrap and let rise in warm place about 30 minutes or until double.

4 Heat oven to 375°. Bake 12 to 15 minutes or until golden brown. Serve warm or cool.

1 Roll: Calories 150 (Calories from Fat 35); Fat 4g (Saturated 2g); Cholesterol 25mg; Sodium 190mg; Carbohydrate 26g (Dietary Fiber 1g); Protein 4g. **Diet Exchanges:** 2 Starch.

Bread Machine Dinner Rolls: Use 3 1/4 cups bread flour, 1/4 cup sugar, 2 tablespoons softened butter, 1 teaspoon salt, 3 teaspoons yeast, 1 cup room-temperature water and 1 egg; omit milk. Measuring carefully, place ingredients in bread machine pan in the order recommended by the manufacturer. Select Dough/Manual cycle; do not use delay cycle. Remove dough from pan. Continue as directed in step 3 for shaping and rising (rising time may be shorter because dough will be warm when removed from bread machine). Bake as directed in step 4.

Do-Ahead Dinner Rolls: After placing rolls in pan, cover tightly with aluminum foil and refrigerate 4 to 24 hours. Before baking, remove from refrigerator; remove foil and cover loosely with plastic wrap. Let rise in warm place about 2 hours or until double (if some rising has occurred in the refrigerator, rising time may be less than 2 hours). Bake as directed in step 4.

Betty's Do-Ahead

You can freeze baked rolls for up to 2 months. To reheat, thaw rolls and warm them, wrapped in aluminum foil, at 275 ° for 10 minutes.

Bread Machine Blueberry Corn Bread

Prep: 10 min   **Cycle:** 3 hr 30 min

1 loaf (1 1/2 pounds), 12 slices

1 cup plus 1 tablespoon water

3 tablespoons molasses or honey

2 tablespoons butter or margarine, softened

3 cups bread flour

1/3 cup yellow cornmeal

1 1/2 teaspoons salt

2 teaspoons bread machine yeast

1/2 cup dried blueberries

1 Make this recipe in bread machines that use 3 cups flour. Measuring carefully, place all ingredients except blueberries in bread machine pan in the order recommended by the manufacturer.

2 Select Basic/White cycle. Use Medium or Light crust color. Do not use delay cycle. Add blueberries at the Raisin/Nut signal or 5 to 10 minutes before last kneading cycle ends. Remove baked bread from pan; cool on wire rack.

1 Slice: Calories 175 (Calories from Fat 20); Fat 2g (Saturated 1g); Cholesterol 5mg; Sodium 310mg; Carbohydrate 37g (Dietary Fiber 2g); Protein 4g. **Diet Exchanges:** 1 1/2 Starch; 1 Fruit.

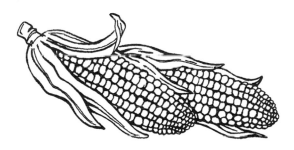

Betty's Simple Substitution

Change the look of this bread by using white cornmeal instead of yellow and replacing the dried blueberries with dried cranberries.

Sweet Potato–Cranberry Knots

Prep: 30 min   **Rise:** 2 hr 10 min   **Bake:** 20 min   **12 rolls**

(see photo insert)

2 1/4 to 2 3/4 cups
bread flour

1/4 cup sugar

1 teaspoon salt

1/2 teaspoon ground
cinnamon

1 package quick active
dry yeast (2 1/4 teaspoons)

1/4 cup butter or
margarine, softened

3/4 cup lukewarm water
(95°)

3/4 cup mashed drained
sweet potatoes packed in
syrup (from 23-ounce can)

1/2 cup dried cranberries

Butter or margarine,
melted

1 Mix 1 cup of the flour, the sugar, salt, cinnamon and yeast in large bowl. Add 1/4 cup butter and the water. Beat with electric mixer on low speed 1 minute, scraping bowl frequently. Add sweet potatoes. Beat on medium speed 1 minute, scraping bowl frequently. Stir in cranberries and enough remaining flour, 1/2 cup at a time, to make dough easy to handle.

2 Place dough on lightly floured surface; gently roll in flour to coat. Knead about 5 minutes or until dough is smooth and springy. Place dough in large bowl greased with shortening, turning dough to grease all sides. Cover bowl loosely with plastic wrap and let rise in warm place 1 hour to 1 hour 30 minutes or until double. Dough is ready if indentation remains when touched.

3 Spray cookie sheet with cooking spray. Gently push fist into dough to deflate. Divide dough into 12 equal pieces. Roll each piece into 8-inch rope; tie into knot. Place on cookie sheet. Brush knots with melted butter. Cover and let rise in warm place about 40 minutes or until double.

4 Heat oven to 375°. Bake 14 to 20 minutes or until golden brown.

1 Roll: Calories 185 (Calories from Fat 45); Fat 5g (Saturated 3g); Cholesterol 15mg; Sodium 240mg; Carbohydrate 32g (Dietary Fiber 2g); Protein 3g. **Diet Exchanges:** 1 Starch, 1 Fruit, 1 Fat.

Betty's
Do-Ahead

Rolls can be made up to a day ahead of time. Reheat in the microwave just before serving. For a citrus twist, add 1 teaspoon freshly grated orange peel with the sweet potatoes.

Praline-Pumpkin-Date Bread

Prep: 15 min   **Bake:** 1 hr   **Cool:** 1 hr 10 min   **2 loaves (24 slices each)**

(see photo insert)

Praline Topping (below)

1 2/3 cups sugar

2/3 cup vegetable oil

2 teaspoons vanilla

4 eggs

1 can (15 ounces) pumpkin (not pumpkin pie mix)

3 cups all-purpose flour

2 teaspoons baking soda

1 teaspoon ground cinnamon

3/4 teaspoon salt

1/2 teaspoon baking powder

1/2 teaspoon ground cloves

1 cup chopped dates

1 Move oven rack to low position so that tops of pans will be in center of oven. Heat oven to 350°. Grease bottoms only of 2 loaf pans, 8 1/2 × 4 1/2 × 2 1/2 inches, or 1 loaf pan, 9 × 5 × 3 inches, with shortening. Make Praline Topping; set aside.

2 Mix sugar, oil, vanilla, eggs and pumpkin in large bowl. Stir in remaining ingredients except dates until well blended. Stir in dates. Pour batter into pans. Sprinkle with topping.

3 Bake 8-inch loaves 50 to 60 minutes, 9-inch loaf 1 hour 10 minutes to 1 hour 20 minutes, or until toothpick inserted in center comes out clean. Cool 10 minutes. Loosen sides of loaves from pans; remove from pans to wire rack. Cool completely, about 1 hour, before slicing.

1 Slice: Calories 110 (Calories from Fat 35); Fat 4g (Saturated 1g); Cholesterol 20mg; Sodium 100mg; Carbohydrate 18g (Dietary Fiber 1g); Protein 2g. **Diet Exchanges:** 1 Starch, 1/2 Fat.

Praline Topping

1/3 cup packed brown sugar

1/3 cup chopped pecans

1 tablespoon butter or margarine, softened

Mix all ingredients until crumbly.

Betty's Do-Ahead

You can wrap the baked loaves tightly and store at room temperature up to 4 days or refrigerate up to 10 days. If traditional pumpkin bread is more to your liking, leave out the topping and the dates.

Savory Sweet Potato Pan Bread

Prep: 15 min   **Bake:** 30 min

10 servings

(see photo insert)

1 1/2 cups uncooked shredded sweet potato (about 1/2 potato)

1/2 cup sugar

1/3 cup vegetable oil

2 eggs

1 cup all-purpose flour

1/2 cup whole wheat flour

2 teaspoons instant minced onion

1 teaspoon dried rosemary leaves, crumbled

1 teaspoon baking soda

1/2 teaspoon salt

1/4 teaspoon baking powder

1 tablespoon sesame seed

1 Heat oven to 350°. Grease bottom only of round pan, 9 × 1 1/2 inches, or square pan, 8 × 8 × 2 inches, with shortening.

2 Mix sweet potato, sugar, oil and eggs in large bowl. Stir in remaining ingredients except sesame seed. Spread in pan. Sprinkle sesame seed over batter.

3 Bake 25 to 30 minutes or until toothpick inserted in center comes out clean. Serve warm.

1 Serving: Calories 220 (Calories from Fat 80); Fat 9g (Saturated 1g); Cholesterol 40mg; Sodium 280mg; Carbohydrate 31g (Dietary Fiber 2g); Protein 4g. **Diet Exchanges:** 2 Starch, 1 1/2 Fat.

Betty's Special Touch

Top off warm wedges of this savory bread with Orange Butter. To make, beat together 1/2 cup softened butter, 1 teaspoon grated orange peel and 1 tablespoon orange juice. If desired, chill about 1 hour to blend flavors.

Surprise Pumpkin Muffins

Prep: 15 min   Bake: 22 min

12 muffins

Cream Cheese Filling
(below)

1/2 cup canned pumpkin
(not pumpkin pie mix)

1/3 cup packed brown
sugar

1/2 cup milk

1/4 cup vegetable oil

2 eggs

1 1/2 cups all-purpose
flour

2 1/2 teaspoons baking
powder

1 teaspoon ground
cinnamon

1/2 teaspoon salt

1/2 teaspoon ground
cloves

1/2 cup chopped nuts

1 Heat oven to 400°. Grease bottoms only of 12 medium muffin cups, 2 1/2 × 1 1/4 inches, or line with paper baking cups. Make Cream Cheese Filling; set aside.

2 Mix pumpkin, brown sugar, milk, oil and eggs in large bowl with spoon. Stir in remaining ingredients except nuts just until flour is moistened. Stir in nuts. Fill muffin cups one-third full. Place about 1 rounded teaspoon filling on batter in each muffin cup. Top with remaining batter.

3 Bake 20 to 22 minutes or until golden brown. Immediately remove from pan to wire rack.

1 Muffin: Calories 210 (Calories from Fat 110); Fat 12g (Saturated 3g); Cholesterol 45mg; Sodium 240mg; Carbohydrate 22g (Dietary Fiber 1g); Protein 4g. **Diet Exchanges:** 1 Starch, 1/2 Fruit, 2 Fat.

Cream Cheese Filling

1 package (3 ounces)
cream cheese, softened

1 tablespoon sugar

1 tablespoon milk

Mix all ingredients until smooth.

Betty's Do-Ahead

You can bake these muffins a day or two ahead of time and freeze. Thaw for 15 minutes at room temperature before serving.

Oatmeal–Cranberry Muffins

Prep: 10 min   **Bake:** 20 min   **12 muffins**

**1 cup buttermilk
or sour milk**

1 cup old-fashioned oats

**1/3 cup butter or
margarine, melted**

**1/2 cup packed brown
sugar**

1 egg

1/4 cup all-purpose flour

**3/4 cup whole wheat
flour**

**1 1/2 teaspoons baking
powder**

1 teaspoon salt

**1 teaspoon ground
cinnamon**

**1 cup fresh or frozen
cranberries, chopped**

1 Heat oven to 400°. Pour buttermilk over oats in small bowl. Grease bottoms only of 12 medium muffin cups, 2 1/2 × 1 1/4 inches, with shortening, or line with paper baking cups.

2 Mix butter, brown sugar and egg in large bowl with spoon. Stir in flours, baking powder, salt and cinnamon just until flour is moistened. Stir in oat mixture; fold in cranberries. Fill muffin cups three-fourths full.

3 Bake 15 to 20 minutes or until golden brown. Immediately remove from pan to wire rack.

1 **Muffin:** Calories 140 (Calories from Fat 45); Fat 5g (Saturated 3g); Cholesterol 30mg; Sodium 330mg; Carbohydrate 20g (Dietary Fiber 2g); Protein 4g. Diet Exchanges: 1 Starch, 1 Fat.

Betty's Simple Substitution

Whole-wheat flour makes this a hearty, grainy muffin. It's less sweet than many muffins, so if you prefer it sweeter, increase brown sugar to 2/3 cup, or sprinkle tops of muffins with a bit of granulated sugar before baking.

Classic Baking Powder Biscuits

Prep: 10 min   **Bake:** 12 min   **12 biscuits**

2 cups all-purpose flour

1 tablespoon sugar

3 teaspoons baking powder

1 teaspoon salt

1/2 cup shortening

About 3/4 cup milk

1 Heat oven to 450°. Mix flour, sugar, baking powder and salt in medium bowl. Cut in shortening, using pastry blender or crisscrossing 2 knives, until mixture looks like fine crumbs. Stir in just enough milk so dough leaves side of bowl and forms a ball (dough will be soft and sticky).

2 Place dough on lightly floured surface; gently roll in flour to coat. Knead lightly 10 times. Roll or pat 1/2 inch thick. Cut with floured 2- to 2 1/4-inch biscuit cutter. Place about 1 inch apart on ungreased cookie sheet for crusty sides, touching for soft sides.

3 Bake 10 to 12 minutes or until golden brown. Immediately remove from cookie sheet. Serve hot.

1 Biscuit: Calories 200 (Calories from Fat 100); Fat 11g (Saturated 3g); Cholesterol 0mg; Sodium 390mg; Carbohydrate 22g (Dietary Fiber 0g); Protein 3g. **Diet Exchanges:** 1 Starch, 1/2 Fruit, 2 Fat.

Buttermilk Biscuits: Decrease baking powder to 2 teaspoons; add 1/4 teaspoon baking soda. Substitute buttermilk for the milk. (If buttermilk is very thick, using slightly more than 3/4 cup may be necessary.)

Betty's Do-Ahead

You can bake these biscuits and freeze, tightly wrapped in foil. About 15 minutes before serving, remove from freezer and heat in foil at 325° for 10 to 12 minutes or until warm.

Angel Biscuits

Prep: 25 min   **Bake:** 14 min

About 15 biscuits

1 package regular or quick active dry yeast (2 1/4 teaspoons)

2 tablespoons warm water (105° to 115°)

2 1/2 cups all-purpose flour

3 tablespoons sugar

1 1/2 teaspoons baking powder

1/2 teaspoon baking soda

1/2 teaspoon salt

1/2 cup shortening

About 1 cup buttermilk

Butter or margarine at room temperature, if desired

1 Heat oven to 400°. Dissolve yeast in warm water; set aside.

2 Mix flour, sugar, baking powder, baking soda and salt in large bowl. Cut in shortening, using pastry blender or crisscrossing 2 knives, until mixture looks like fine crumbs. Stir in yeast mixture and just enough buttermilk so dough leaves side of bowl and forms a ball.

3 Place dough on generously floured surface; gently roll in flour to coat. Knead lightly 25 to 30 times, sprinkling with flour if dough is too sticky. Roll or pat 1/2 inch thick. Cut with floured 2 1/2-inch biscuit cutter. Place about 1 inch apart on ungreased cookie sheet.

4 Bake 12 to 14 minutes or until golden brown. Immediately remove from cookie sheet. Brush with butter. Serve hot.

1 Biscuit: Calories 145 (Calories from Fat 65); Fat 7g (Saturated 2g); Cholesterol 0mg; Sodium 180mg; Carbohydrate 19g (Dietary Fiber 1g); Protein 3g. **Diet Exchanges:** 1 Starch, 1 Fat.

Betty's Special Touch

Yeast makes these biscuits light as angels! If you have time, you can make them even lighter. Just cover unbaked biscuits and let rise in a warm place for about 30 minutes or until puffy. Bake as directed.

Southeast Favorites

Serves 10

Because animals and crops thrived in the warm southern climate, corn, sweet potatoes and pork became mainstays of the cooking style. Fried chicken and hot biscuits are distinctly southern traditions, as are sweet potato and pecan pies.

Cajun Deep-Fried Turkey, page 28
or Grilled Lemon-Herb Turkey, page 26
Baked Ham with Zesty Cranberry Sauce, page 95
Corn Bread Stuffing, page 52
Milk Gravy, page 50 or No-Drippings Gravy, page 49
Classic Mashed Potatoes, page 71
Creamy Confetti Succotash, page 85
Angel Biscuits, above
Sweet Potato Pie, page 159
Brandy Pecan Pie, page 165

Sweet Potato Biscuits

Prep: 15 min   **Bake:** 15 min

About 12 biscuits

2 cups all-purpose flour

1/4 cup sugar

2 1/2 teaspoons baking powder

1 teaspoon salt

1/2 cup shortening

1 cup mashed cooked sweet potatoes

1/2 cup milk

1 Heat oven to 450°. Mix flour, sugar, baking powder and salt in large bowl. Cut in shortening, using pastry blender or crisscrossing 2 knives, until mixture looks like fine crumbs. Mix sweet potatoes and milk; stir into flour mixture until soft dough forms.

2 Place dough on generously floured surface; gently roll in flour to coat. Knead gently 10 times. Roll or pat 3/4 inch thick. Cut with floured 2 1/4-inch biscuit cutter. Place about 1 inch apart on ungreased cookie sheet.

3 Bake 12 to 15 minutes or until light golden brown.

1 Biscuit: Calories 195 (Calories from Fat 80); Fat 9g (Saturated 2g); Cholesterol 0mg; Sodium 310mg; Carbohydrate 26g (Dietary Fiber 1g); Protein 3g. **Diet Exchanges:** 1 Starch, 1 Fruit, 1 Fat.

Bisquick Mix Sweet Potato Biscuits: Substitute 2 1/2 cups Original Bisquick mix for the flour and 1/3 cup butter or margarine, softened, for the shortening; omit sugar, baking powder and salt. Stir Bisquick, butter, sweet potatoes and milk until soft dough forms. Place dough on surface dusted with Bisquick and roll to coat. Shape into a ball; knead 3 or 4 times. Roll 1/2 inch thick. Cut with 2 1/4 inch cutter dipped in Bisquick. Place with edges touching on ungreased cookie sheet. Bake at 450° for 10 to 12 minutes or until golden brown. About 16 biscuits.

Betty's Do-Ahead

Be ready to prepare these easy biscuits anytime by cooking sweet potatoes ahead: Simmer sweet potatoes, covered, 20 to 25 minutes or until tender when pierced with a fork; drain. When potatoes are cool enough to handle, slip off skins and mash until no lumps remain. You can also use mashed cooked squash in place of the sweet potatoes.

Golden Carrot-Spice Scones

Prep: 15 min   **Bake:** 18 min

10 scones

2 cups all-purpose flour

1/4 cup sugar

2 1/2 teaspoons baking
powder

1 teaspoon pumpkin pie
spice

1/2 teaspoon salt

1/3 cup firm butter
or margarine

1/3 cup milk

1 cup finely shredded
carrots (1 1/2 medium)

1/2 cup golden raisins

1 egg

Spice Glaze (below)

1 Heat oven to 400°. Mix flour, sugar, baking powder, pumpkin pie spice and salt in large bowl. Cut in butter, using pastry blender or crisscrossing 2 knives, until mixture looks like fine crumbs. Stir in milk, carrots, raisins and egg until dough leaves side of bowl and forms a ball.

2 Drop dough by tablespoonfuls 2 inches apart onto ungreased cookie sheet; press slightly.

3 Bake 15 to 18 minutes or until light golden brown. Immediately remove from cookie sheet to wire rack. Drizzle with Spice Glaze. Serve warm.

1 Scone: Calories 240 (Calories from Fat 70); Fat 8g (Saturated 5g); Cholesterol 40mg; Sodium 300mg; Carbohydrate 38g (Dietary Fiber 1g); Protein 4g. **Diet Exchanges:** 1 1/2 Starch, 1 Fruit, 1 1/2 Fat.

Spice Glaze

1/2 cup powdered sugar

2 tablespoons milk

1/8 teaspoon pumpkin
pie spice or ground cin-
namon

Mix all ingredients until smooth.

Betty's Simple Substitution

If you don't have pumpkin pie spice on hand, you can make your own by mixing 1/2 teaspoon ground cinnamon, 1/4 teaspoon ground ginger, 1/8 teaspoon ground nutmeg and 1/8 teaspoon ground cloves. Make wedge-shaped scones by patting dough into a circle and cutting into wedges before baking.

Southern Buttermilk Corn Bread

Prep: 10 min   **Bake:** 30 min

12 servings

1 1/2 cups yellow, white or blue cornmeal

1/2 cup all-purpose flour

1 1/2 cups buttermilk

1/4 cup vegetable oil

2 teaspoons baking powder

1 teaspoon sugar

1 teaspoon salt

1/2 teaspoon baking soda

2 eggs or 1/2 cup fat-free cholesterol-free egg product or 4 egg whites

1 Heat oven to 450°. Grease bottom and side of round pan, 9 × 1 1/2 inches, or square pan, 8 × 8 × 2 inches, with shortening. Mix all ingredients with spoon until blended. Beat vigorously 30 seconds. Pour batter into pan.

2 Bake 25 to 30 minutes or until golden brown. Serve warm.

1 Serving: Calories 145 (Calories from Fat 55); Fat 6g (Saturated 1g); Cholesterol 35mg; Sodium 370mg; Carbohydrate 19g (Dietary Fiber 1g); Protein 4g. **Diet Exchanges:** 1 1/2 Starch.

Betty's Helpful Tip

This corn bread is great served as a traditional bread for your Thanksgiving meal, or make it a day or two before and use it in Corn Bread Stuffing, page 00. It makes 9 1/2 cups of cubed corn bread.

Soups *and* Salads

Sausage–Cheese Balls

Prep: 10 min   **Bake:** 25 min   **About 8 1/2 dozen appetizers**

3 cups Original Bisquick

1 pound uncooked bulk pork sausage

4 cups shredded Cheddar cheese (16 ounces)

1/2 cup grated Parmesan cheese

1/2 cup milk

1/2 teaspoon dried rosemary leaves, crumbled

1 1/2 teaspoons chopped fresh parsley or 1/2 teaspoon parsley flakes

1 Heat oven to 350°. Spray jelly roll pan, 15 1/2 × 10 1/2 × 1 inch, with cooking spray.

2 Stir all ingredients until well mixed (you may need to use your hands). Shape mixture into 1-inch balls. Place in pan.

3 Bake 20 to 25 minutes or until brown. Immediately remove from pan. Serve warm.

1 **Serving (2 Appetizers):** Calories 80 (Calories from Fat 45); Fat 5g (Saturated 3g); Cholesterol 15mg; Sodium 220mg; Carbohydrate 4g (Dietary Fiber 0g); Protein 4g. **Diet Exchanges:** 1/2 High-Fat Meat, 1/2 Fat.

Ham Balls: Substitute 1 1/2 cups finely chopped fully cooked ham for the sausage. Omit rosemary. Increase milk to 2/3 cup and use 1/2 cup chopped fresh parsley or 2 tablespoons parsley flakes. Mix and bake as directed.

Betty's Do-Ahead

Make these bite-sized appetizers up to a day ahead of time and refrigerate; bake as directed. Or cover and freeze unbaked balls up to 1 month. Bake frozen balls 25 to 30 minutes or until brown.

Marvelous Munchies

Though most of the day's attention is centered around the big feast, your guests will appreciate these savory snacks to "tide them over."

- **Celery Stuffers:** Stir 1 teaspoon chili powder and 1 tablespoon Worcestershire sauce into 8 ounces cream cheese. Fill celery sticks; sprinkle with 4 ounces toasted pumpkin seeds (page 157) or sunflower nuts.
- **Fall Fruit Dip:** Stir 2 tablespoons brown sugar and 1 teaspoon ground cinnamon into 8 ounces plain yogurt. Dip apple and pear slices or any fall fruits.
- **Bell Pepper Nachos:** Sprinkle shredded mozzarella or Monterey Jack cheese over slices of yellow, orange or green bell peppers; melt cheese in microwave.
- **Chutney and Cream:** Top cream cheese with chilled Cranberry-Pistachio Sauce (page 105), Apple-Cranberry Chutney (page 64) or purchased cranberry or apple chutney. Sprinkle with chopped pistachio nuts, and serve with crackers.
- **Nuts about Cheese and Crackers:** Cut Cheddar, Colby-Monterey Jack and mozzarella cheeses with leaf-shaped cookie cutters. Overlap "leaves" on platter; sprinkle whole or halved hazelnuts on top to look like acorns. Serve with crackers and chutney.
- **Relish Tray:** Assemble several kinds of olives, radishes, baby carrots, baby pickles or other favorites on a platter or in several small bowls on a tray. Cover and refrigerate until serving.
- **Cucumber Nibbles:** Spread cucumber or zucchini slices with mayonnaise; top with smoked salmon or imitation crabmeat.
- **Creamy Maple-Nut Spread:** Mix cream cheese and maple syrup; stir in chopped nuts. Serve with sliced French bread, crackers, apples or pears.

Snacking Savvy

- Serve dips in a hollowed onion or red pepper for extra pizzazz.
- If you have special platters, like a marble cheese board or silver trays, pull them out for this special holiday celebration.
- Baskets lined with parchment paper or pretty dishtowels can hold sliced bread or cut-up veggies for dips.

Savory Pecans

Prep: 5 min   **Bake:** 10 min

8 servings (1/4 cup each)

2 cups pecan halves

2 medium green onions, chopped (2 tablespoons)

2 tablespoons butter or margarine, melted

1 tablespoon soy sauce

1/4 teaspoon ground red pepper (cayenne)

1 Heat oven to 300°. Mix all ingredients. Spread pecans in single layer in ungreased jelly roll pan, 15 1/2 × 10 1/2 × 1 inch.

2 Bake uncovered about 10 minutes or until pecans are toasted. Serve warm, or cool completely. Store in airtight container at room temperature up to 3 weeks.

1/4 Cup: Calories 225 (Calories from Fat 200); Fat 22g (Saturated 3g); Cholesterol 10mg; Sodium 135mg; Carbohydrate 4g (Dietary Fiber 3g); Protein 3g. **Diet Exchanges:** 1/2 High-Fat Meat, 4 Fat.

Spiced Pecans: Omit the ground red pepper, and stir in 2 teaspoons five-spice powder and 1/2 teaspoon ground ginger.

Tex-Mex Pecans: Omit soy sauce and ground red pepper, and stir in 1 tablespoon Worcestershire sauce, 2 teaspoons chili powder, 1/4 teaspoon garlic salt and 1/4 teaspoon onion powder.

Betty's Simple Substitution

Walnut halves or peanuts can be used instead of the pecans. Keep these delicious snacking nuts on hand as extra nibbles for parties.

Pork Crown Roast with
Cranberry Stuffing (page 96)

*Marinated Beef Tenderloin
with Merlot Sauce* (page 98)

Sweet Potato–Cranberry Knots (page 114)

Praline-Pumpkin-Date Bread (page 115)

Savory Sweet Potato Pan Bread (page 116)

Nutty Squash Pie (page 160)

Cranberry-Raspberry Bread Pudding (page 167)

Slow Cooker Pumpkin-Apple Dessert (page 170)

Oyster Stew

Prep: 10 min   **Cook:** 10 min

4 servings

1/4 cup butter or margarine

1 pint shucked oysters, undrained

2 cups milk

1/2 cup half-and-half

1/2 teaspoon salt

Dash of pepper

1 Melt butter in 1 1/2-quart saucepan over low heat. Stir in oysters (with liquid). Cook, stirring occasionally, just until edges curl.

2 Heat milk and half-and-half in 2-quart saucepan over medium-low heat until hot. Stir in salt, pepper and oyster mixture; heat until hot.

1 **Serving:** Calories 285 (Calories from Fat 180); Fat 20g (Saturated 12g); Cholesterol 115mg; Sodium 710mg; Carbohydrate 12g (Dietary Fiber 0g); Protein 14g. **Diet Exchanges:** 1 Medium-Fat Meat, 3 Fat, 1 Skim Milk.

Microwave Oyster Stew: Place butter in a 2-quart microwavable casserole. Microwave uncovered on High 30 to 60 seconds or until melted. Stir in oysters (with liquid). Microwave uncovered 4 minutes, stirring after 2 minutes. Stir in remaining ingredients. Microwave uncovered 3 to 6 minutes longer or until hot.

Betty's Helpful Tip

Use your microwave as much as you can to free up your oven and the stovetop for other dishes. It's perfect for heating this easy first course while the turkey rests before carving and the sides are heating.

Easy Gingered Pumpkin Soup

Prep: 10 min   **Cook:** 18 min   **5 servings**

**1 tablespoon olive
or vegetable oil**

**1 medium onion, finely
chopped (1/2 cup)**

**2 teaspoons grated
gingerroot**

**1 clove garlic,
finely chopped**

3 cups water

1/8 teaspoon pepper

**2 vegetarian vegetable
or chicken bouillon cubes**

**1 can (15 ounces) pumpkin
(not pumpkin pie mix)**

1 Heat oil in 3-quart saucepan over medium-high heat. Cook onion, gingerroot and garlic in oil 2 minutes, stirring frequently.

2 Stir in remaining ingredients. Heat to boiling; reduce heat. Cover and simmer 15 to 18 minutes, stirring frequently, to blend flavors.

1 Serving: Calories 65 (Calories from Fat 25); Fat 3g (Saturated 1g); Cholesterol 0mg; Sodium 470mg; Carbohydrate 9g (Dietary Fiber 3g); Protein 1g. **Diet Exchanges:** 1/2 Fruit, 1/2 Fat.

Betty's Simple Substitution

The Pilgrims would have loved the rich blend of flavors in this simple, hearty soup. Instead of the canned pumpkin, you can use 2 cups cooked fresh pumpkin or a 16-ounce bag of frozen (thawed) squash.

Acorn Squash and Apple Soup

Prep: 20 min   **Bake:** 40 min   **Cook:** 40 min   **6 servings**

**1 medium acorn squash
(1 1/2 to 2 pounds)**

**2 tablespoons butter
or margarine**

**1 medium yellow onion,
sliced**

**2 medium tart cooking
apples (Granny Smith,
Greening or Haralson),
peeled and sliced**

**1 teaspoon dried thyme
leaves**

**1/4 teaspoon dried basil
leaves**

**2 cans (14 ounces each)
chicken broth (4 cups)**

1/2 cup half-and-half

**1 teaspoon ground
nutmeg**

1/2 teaspoon salt

**1/4 teaspoon white
or black pepper**

1 Heat oven to 350°. Cut squash in half; remove seeds and fibers. Place squash, cut sides up, in rectangular pan, 13 × 9 × 2 inches. Pour water into pan until 1/4 inch deep. Bake uncovered about 40 minutes or until tender. Cool; remove pulp from rind and set aside.

2 Melt butter in heavy 3-quart saucepan over medium heat. Cook onion in butter 2 to 3 minutes, stirring occasionally, until crisp-tender. Stir in apples, thyme and basil. Cook 2 minutes, stirring constantly. Stir in broth. Heat to boiling; reduce heat to low. Simmer uncovered 30 minutes.

3 Remove 1 cup apples with slotted spoon; set aside. Place one-third of the remaining apple mixture and squash in blender or food processor. Cover and blend on medium speed about 1 minute or until smooth; pour into bowl. Continue to blend in small batches until all the soup is pureed.

4 Return blended mixture and 1 cup reserved apples to saucepan. Stir in half and half, nutmeg, salt and pepper; heat until hot.

1 Serving: Calories 155 (Calories from Fat 65); Fat 7g (Saturated 4g); Cholesterol 15mg; Sodium 910mg; Carbohydrate 20g (Dietary Fiber 2g); Protein 5g. **Diet Exchanges:** 2 Vegetable, 1/2 Fruit, 1 1/2 Fat.

Betty's Simple Substitution

If you love squash, you'll love this hearty and tasty soup. Butternut or butter-cup squash can be used instead of the acorn squash.

Vegetarian Thanksgiving Dinner

Serves 10

If you decide to have a vegetarian feast this year for a change, whether it's to please a guest, for health reasons or just to celebrate the glories of the harvest, you'll find plenty of delicious options. The rich fall flavors in this meal will delight vegetarians and nonvegetarians alike. With all of these tempting seasonal suggestions, no one will miss the turkey!

Orange-Cranberry-Pecan Salad, page 145
Acorn Squash and Apple Soup, above
Chestnut Stuffing, page 52
Roasted-Vegetable Lasagna, page 107
Spicy Fruit Compote, page 63
Savory Sweet Potato Pan Bread, page 116
Crimson Crumble Bars, page 172
Pumpkin Cheesecake, page 158

Sweet Potato Soup

Prep: 15 min   **Cook:** 45 min

4 servings

2 large dark-orange sweet potatoes (1 1/2 pounds)

1 cup chicken broth

1/4 cup orange juice

1/4 teaspoon salt

1/4 teaspoon ground nutmeg

1 cup milk

1/4 cup chopped pecans

Additional ground nutmeg, if desired

1 Heat enough water to cover sweet potatoes to boiling in 2-quart saucepan. Add sweet potatoes. Cover and heat to boiling; reduce heat. Simmer 30 to 35 minutes or until potatoes are tender when pierced with a fork; drain. When potatoes are cool enough to handle, slip off skins; discard skins.

2 Place potatoes in blender or food processor. Add 1/2 cup of the broth. Cover and blend on medium speed until smooth.

3 Return blended mixture to saucepan. Stir in remaining broth, the orange juice, salt and 1/4 teaspoon nutmeg. Cook over medium-high heat, stirring constantly, until hot. Stir in milk. Cook, stirring frequently, until hot. Sprinkle with pecans and additional nutmeg.

1 Serving: Calories 195 (Calories from Fat 65); Fat 7g (Saturated 1g); Cholesterol 5mg; Sodium 440mg; Carbohydrate 27g (Dietary Fiber 3g); Protein 6g. **Diet Exchanges:** 1 ½ Starch, 1 Vegetable, 1 Fat.

Betty's Simple Substitution

You may omit step 1 by using a 23-ounce can of sweet potatoes in place of the fresh sweet potatoes. Be sure to add the juices from the can with the potatoes to make the soup more flavorful.

Golden Vegetable Chowder

Prep: 12 min   **Cook:** 15 min

6 servings

**1 tablespoon butter
or margarine**

**1 medium green bell
pepper, coarsely chopped
(1 cup)**

**1 medium red bell pepper,
coarsely chopped (1 cup)**

**8 medium green onions,
sliced (1/2 cup)**

3 cups water

**3/4 pound new potatoes,
cut into 1-inch pieces
(2 1/2 cups)**

**1 tablespoon chopped
fresh or 1 teaspoon dried
thyme leaves**

1/2 teaspoon salt

1 cup half-and-half

1/8 teaspoon pepper

**2 cans (14 3/4 ounces
each) cream-style corn**

1 Melt butter in 4-quart Dutch oven over medium heat. Cook bell peppers and onions in butter 3 minutes, stirring occasionally.

2 Stir in water, potatoes, thyme and salt. Heat to boiling; reduce heat to low. Cover and simmer about 10 minutes or until potatoes are tender.

3 Stir in remaining ingredients. Heat until hot (do not boil).

1 Serving: Calories 250 (Calories from Fat 70); Fat 8g (Saturated 4g); Cholesterol 20mg; Sodium 540mg; Carbohydrate 43g (Dietary Fiber 5g); Protein 7g. **Diet Exchanges:** 2 Starch, 2 Vegetable, 1 Fat.

Betty's Simple Substitution

Step into the fall season by cooking with harvest-colored vegetables. Use orange and yellow bell peppers in place of the red and green peppers, and use Yukon gold potatoes in place of the new potatoes.

Fall Fruit and Pasta Salad

Prep: 15 min   **Chill:** 30 min   **8 servings**

1 cup uncooked small
pasta shells (4 ounces)

1 medium unpeeled
red eating apple (Gala,
Cortland, Delicious or
Braeburn), chopped
(1 1/4 cups)

1 medium unpeeled pear,
chopped (1 1/4 cups)

4 medium green onions,
chopped (1/4 cup)

1/4 cup chopped pecans

1/4 cup dried cranberries

1/3 cup mayonnaise
or salad dressing

3 tablespoons orange
marmalade

1/2 teaspoon dried
marjoram leaves

1/4 teaspoon salt

1 Cook and drain pasta as directed on package. Rinse with cold water; drain.

2 Mix pasta, apple, pear, onions, pecans and cranberries in large glass or plastic bowl. Mix remaining ingredients; stir into pasta mixture.

3 Cover and refrigerate at least 30 minutes until chilled.

1 Serving: Calories 200 (Calories from Fat 90); Fat 10g (Saturated 1g); Cholesterol 5mg; Sodium 130mg; Carbohydrate 26g (Dietary Fiber 2g); Protein 3g. **Diet Exchanges:** 1 Starch, 1 Fruit, 1 1/2 Fat.

Betty's Simple Substitution

Combine pasta and fruit
for a delicious side dish—
dried cherries, dried blueberries or raisins can be
used instead of the dried
cranberries.

Make and Take

Certain foods are better travelers than others. Of course, much depends on the distance traveled, how the food is packed and what food you are taking. If you plan to take food on the road, consider some of these easy totables.

- **Completely prepared foods** that don't need to be kept hot or cold are ideal travelers. Try snack mixes, rolls, breads, biscuits, muffins, cookies and bars.
- **Salads or side dishes,** such as Classic Green Bean Casserole (page 69), can be assembled at the host's house. If you're traveling several hours, take the ingredients (cans of green beans, cream of mushroom soup, French-fried onions and your casserole dish). When you arrive at your host's house, assemble and bake it there
- **Salads** can be made ahead of time and chilled. Place tightly covered salad in a cooler, along with an ice pack. Pack dressing in a separate container.
- **Cranberry or other sauces** can be made ahead of time and chilled. Place tightly covered sauce in a cooler, along with an ice pack.
- **Casseroles and side dishes** that are completely baked and cooled can be tightly wrapped and chilled. Check ahead of time to make sure there's oven space, if you need it. And allow plenty of extra time (refer to recipe) to heat once you arrive at your destination.
- **Casseroles and side dishes** that are completely baked and covered will keep warm, if you are traveling 20 minutes or less.
- **Beverages** packaged in individual or large-size containers, such as soda, water or wine are usually welcome.
- **Pies** filled with fruit or nuts don't need to be kept hot or cold.
- **Cakes** baked and frosted in a rectangular pan or unfrosted cakes like bundt cakes are the best travelers. If taking extra sauce or topping for a cake, place it in a separate container.

Refrigerated Fruit Salad

Prep: 10 min   **Chill:** 4 hr

12 servings

1 can (21 ounces) peach or apricot pie filling

1 can (20 ounces) pineapple chunks in unsweetened juice, drained

1 can (11 ounces) mandarin orange segments, drained

1 cup seedless red or green grapes, cut in half

1 cup miniature marshmallows

2 bananas, sliced

1 Mix all ingredients in large bowl.

2 Cover and refrigerate at least 4 hours but no longer than 24 hours.

1 Serving: Calories 130 (Calories from Fat 0); Fat 0g (Saturated 0g); Cholesterol 0mg; Sodium 5mg; Carbohydrate 32g (Dietary Fiber 1g); Protein 1g. **Diet Exchanges:** 2 Fruit.

Betty's Simple Substitution

Perhaps you'll remember this long-time favorite from your childhood. This golden-colored, very fall-looking salad is great to make ahead. You can substitute a 15-ounce can of fruit cocktail, drained, for the pineapple.

So-Simple Cranberry Gelatin Salad

Prep: 10 min   **Chill:** 6 hr

2 tubs (12 ounces each) cranberry-orange sauce

1 tub (12 ounces) cranberry-raspberry sauce

2 cups boiling water

1 package (6 ounces) lemon-flavored gelatin

1 Lightly brush 6 1/2-cup ring mold with vegetable oil. Mix cranberry sauces in large bowl.

2 Pour boiling water on gelatin in small bowl; stir until gelatin is dissolved. Stir gelatin into cranberry sauces; pour into mold. Cover and refrigerate at least 6 hours but no longer than 24 hours.

3 To unmold salad, dip mold into hot water for 10 seconds. Place serving plate upside down onto mold; turn plate and mold over, then remove mold. Refrigerate salad until serving.

1 Serving: Calories 205 (Calories from Fat 0); Fat 0g (Saturated 0g); Cholesterol 0mg; Sodium 60mg; Carbohydrate 50g (Dietary Fiber 2g); Protein 1g. **Diet Exchanges:** 3 1/2 Fruit.

Betty's Special Touch

Add a little flair by garnishing the center of the salad with sprigs of watercress and some fresh or frozen (thawed) cranberries.

Cranberry-Orange Gelatin Salad

Prep: 20 min   **Freeze:** 15 min   **Chill:** 30 min   **12 servings**

1 can (20 ounces) crushed pineapple in juice

2 packages (3 ounces each) cranberry-flavored gelatin

14 ice cubes

2 cups fresh or frozen cranberries

1 unpeeled seedless orange, cut into 1-inch pieces

Additional fresh cranberries, orange slices and mint sprigs, if desired

Creamy Topping (below), if desired

1 Drain pineapple, reserving juice in 4-cup measuring cup; set pineapple aside. Add enough water to pineapple juice to measure 2 1/2 cups; pour into 1-quart saucepan. Heat to boiling.

2 Place gelatin in rectangular baking dish, 11 × 7 × 1 1/2 inches (2-quart size). Add boiling juice mixture; stir until gelatin is completely dissolved. Add ice cubes; stir until ice is completely melted and gelatin begins to thicken. Place in freezer 10 to 15 minutes, stirring once or twice, until slightly thickened.

3 Meanwhile, place 2 cups cranberries and the orange in food processor. Cover and process until coarsely chopped; set aside.

4 Remove gelatin from freezer. Stir cranberry mixture and pineapple into gelatin. Cover with plastic wrap and refrigerate at least 30 minutes until firm. Garnish with cranberries, orange slices and mint. Serve with Creamy Topping.

1 **Serving:** Calories 125 (Calories from Fat 0); Fat 0g (Saturated 0g); Cholesterol 0mg; Sodium 50mg; Carbohydrate 28g (Dietary Fiber 1g); Protein 3g. **Diet Exchanges:** 2 Fruit.

Creamy Topping

2/3 cup vanilla yogurt

1/3 cup reduced-fat sour cream

Mix yogurt and sour cream in small bowl until blended. Cover and refrigerate until serving.

Betty's Helpful Tip

Canned pineapple is the best option for this easy molded fruit salad. The gelatin will not set up if you use fresh or frozen pineapple.

Lime, Pineapple and Carrot Salad

Prep: 15 min   **Chill:** 5 hr   **6 servings**

1 cup boiling water

1 package (3 ounces) lime- or lemon-flavored gelatin

1/2 cup cold water

1 can (8 ounces) crushed pineapple, undrained

1/2 cup shredded carrot

Mayonnaise or whipped cream, if desired

1 Pour boiling water on gelatin in medium bowl; stir until gelatin is dissolved. Stir in cold water and pineapple. Refrigerate about 45 minutes or until thickened but not set.

2 Lightly brush six 1/2-cup salad molds with vegetable oil. Stir carrot into thickened gelatin; pour into molds. Refrigerate about 4 hours or until firm.

3 To unmold salads, dip molds into hot water for 10 seconds. Place salad plate upside down onto each mold; turn plate and mold over, then remove mold. Top salads with mayonnaise.

1 Serving: Calories 80 (Calories from Fat 0); Fat 0g (Saturated 0g); Cholesterol 0mg; Sodium 40mg; Carbohydrate 20g (Dietary Fiber 1g); Protein 1g. **Diet Exchanges:** 1 1/2 Fruit.

Betty's Simple Substitution

This recipe can be made with any fruit or vegetable combination. Try 1 cup fruit cocktail in place of the pineapple and 1/2 cup chopped celery or green bell pepper instead of the carrot.

Layered Vegetable Salad

Prep: 25 min   **Cook:** 12 min   **Chill:** 4 hr   **6 servings**

1 cup diced peeled beets (about 2 medium)

1 1/2 cups broccoli flowerets

1/2 cup reduced-fat ranch dressing

1 medium yellow bell pepper, cut into thin 1-inch strips (1 cup)

1 medium green bell pepper, cut into thin 1-inch strips (1 cup)

1/2 cup thinly sliced halved red onion

1 can (14 ounces) artichoke hearts, drained and cut into fourths

1 cup shredded reduced-fat Cheddar cheese (4 ounces)

1 Place beets in 1 1/2-quart saucepan; add just enough water to cover beets. Heat to boiling; reduce heat to low. Cover and simmer 8 to 12 minutes or until beets are tender; drain. Rinse with cold water; drain.

2 Layer broccoli, 1/4 cup of the dressing, the yellow bell pepper, cooked beets, green bell pepper, onion and artichokes in 1 1/2-quart glass bowl. Top with cheese. Cover and refrigerate at least 4 hours but no longer than 24 hours.

3 Just before serving, top with remaining 1/4 cup dressing. To serve, use long-handled serving spoons to reach all layers.

1 **Serving:** Calories 135 (Calories from Fat 55); Fat 6g (Saturated 1g); Cholesterol 5mg; Sodium 680mg; Carbohydrate 16g (Dietary Fiber 5g); Protein 9g. **Diet Exchanges:** 3 Vegetable, 1 Fat.

Betty's Simple Substitution

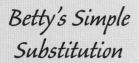

This colorful salad is best made the evening before your big meal. To make preparation easier, use a 16-ounce can of sliced beets, thoroughly drained, instead of cooking fresh beets.

Festive Fall Coleslaw

Prep: 15 min

12 servings

**Orange and Lemon
Vinaigrette (below)**

**1 bag (16 ounces)
coleslaw mix**

**1/2 green bell pepper,
cut into small thin strips
(1/2 cup)**

**1/2 yellow bell pepper,
cut into small thin strips
(1/2 cup)**

**1/2 orange bell pepper,
cut into small thin strips
(1/2 cup)**

1 Make Orange and Lemon Vinaigrette.

2 Mix remaining ingredients in large bowl. Pour vinaigrette over coleslaw mixture; toss.

---

1 Serving: Calories 150 (Calories from Fat 110); Fat 12g (Saturated 1g); Cholesterol 0mg; Sodium 105mg; Carbohydrate 9g (Dietary Fiber 1g); Protein 1g. **Diet Exchanges:** 2 Vegetable, 2 Fat.

Orange and Lemon Vinaigrette

1/3 cup sugar

1/4 cup orange juice

**2 tablespoons lemon
juice**

1/2 teaspoon salt

**1/2 teaspoon onion
powder**

**1/2 teaspoon ground
mustard**

2/3 cup vegetable oil

Beat all ingredients except oil in medium bowl with wire whisk until blended. Gradually beat in oil until blended.

Betty's Simple Substitution

This is a delightful twist on traditional coleslaw. If you run out of time, omit the vinaigrette and use 2/3 cup coleslaw dressing, or mix 2/3 cup mayonnaise and 3 tablespoons milk, then stir into coleslaw mixture.

Soups and Salads • 141

Dried Cherry, Walnut and Gorgonzola Salad

Prep: 15 min

4 servings

1 tablespoon white wine vinegar

2 teaspoons mayonnaise or salad dressing

1/2 teaspoon Dijon mustard

1/4 teaspoon salt

Dash of pepper

3 tablespoons olive or vegetable oil

1 bag (10 ounces) romaine and leaf lettuce salad mix (about 4 cups)

1/2 cup dried cherries

1/2 cup crumbled Gorgonzola cheese (2 ounces)

1/2 cup coarsely chopped walnuts

1 Beat vinegar, mayonnaise, mustard, salt and pepper in small bowl with wire whisk until blended. Gradually beat in oil until well blended. Cover and refrigerate until serving.

2 Just before serving, place lettuce in large bowl. Pour dressing over lettuce; toss. Divide lettuce among serving plates. Sprinkle with cherries, cheese and walnuts.

1 Serving: Calories 220 (Calories from Fat 305); Fat 26g (Saturated 5g); Cholesterol 10mg; Sodium 390mg; Carbohydrate 17g (Dietary Fiber 3g); Protein 7g. **Diet Exchanges:** 2 Vegetable, 1/2 Fruit, 5 Fat.

Betty's Do-Ahead

Make the dressing for this quick and elegant salad a day ahead of time; cover and refrigerate. Toss lettuce with the dressing just before serving.

Northwest Favorites

Serves 18

The melding of diverse immigrants (Spanish, Mexican, Russian, Swiss, Portuguese and Italian), and Native American inhabitants makes the foods of these states especially rich and varied. Fruit-tree seedlings carried across the Oregon Trail by settlers became the basis for the region's well-known produce: apples, pears, plums, walnuts and filberts.

Dried Cherry, Walnut and Gorgonzola Salad, above
Slow Cooker Turkey Breast
Stuffed with Wild Rice and Cranberries, page 36
No-Drippings Gravy, page 49
Spicy Fruit Compote, page 63
Wild Rice–Pecan Stuffing, page 54
Classic Baked Corn Pudding, page 83
Whole Wheat Dinner Rolls and Butter
Nutty Squash Pie, page 160
Harvest Upside-Down Cake, page 171

Classic Waldorf Salad

Prep: 10 min

4 servings

1/2 cup mayonnaise
or salad dressing

1 tablespoon lemon juice

1 tablespoon milk

2 medium unpeeled red
eating apples, coarsely
chopped (2 cups)

2 medium stalks celery,
chopped (1 cup)

1/3 cup coarsely chopped
nuts

Salad greens, if desired

1 Mix mayonnaise, lemon juice and milk in medium bowl.

2 Stir in apples, celery and nuts. Serve on salad greens.

1 Serving: Calories 305 (Calories from Fat 250); Fat 28g (Saturated 4g); Cholesterol 15mg; Sodium 180mg; Carbohydrate 14g (Dietary Fiber 3g); Protein 2g. **Diet Exchanges:** 1 Fruit, 5 Fat.

Gingered Apple-Cranberry Salad: Mix 2 1/2 cups cubed red apples, 1/2 cup chopped celery and 1/4 cup sweetened dried cranberries in large bowl. Mix 1/4 cup reduced-calorie mayonnaise, 1 tablespoon orange juice and 1 teaspoon grated gingerroot in small bowl. Gently stir dressing into salad.

Betty's Simple Substitution

Instead of apples, why not try fresh pears? Stirring in 2 tablespoons of dried blueberries, cherries, cranberries or raisins is perfect for adding tasty flavor and a pretty burst of color.

— *All About* — Apples

Q. **There are so many apple varieties— how do I choose one?**

A. When it comes to choosing the right apple, there are plenty of tasty possibilities! Here's a handy guide to some of the most popular and best tasting varieties.

Braeburn Yellow-skinned with red blush; crisp, juicy, sweet and tart. Great for fresh salads, baking whole and making into delicious applesauce.

Granny Smith Pale green and very tart; crisp and firm. The hard flesh makes it a good choice for pies, crisps and cobblers.

Ida Red Large and bright red; firm, crisp and juicy. Especially good for snacks and desserts; the firm quality makes great pies and crisps.

McIntosh Red-on-green color; crisp, juicy and slightly perfumed. Excellent fresh, they work well for sauce, but they collapse when baked whole or in pies.

Rome Beauty Large, deep red; sweet, mildly tart and firm. Ideal for baking whole and in pies or crisps because they retain shape and flavor.

Citrus Fruit Salad

Prep: 20 min

6 servings

Orange-Honey Dressing (below)

1/2 medium jicama, peeled and cut into 1/4-inch slices

3 medium oranges, peeled and sliced

3 medium kiwifruit, peeled and sliced

1/4 cup dried cranberries

1 Make Orange-Honey Dressing.

2 Cut jicama slices into star shapes, using small star-shaped cookie cutter.

3 Mix jicama, oranges and kiwifruit in serving bowl. Toss with dressing. Top with cranberries.

1 Serving: Calories 130 (Calories from Fat 0); Fat 0g (Saturated 0g); Cholesterol 0mg; Sodium 5mg; Carbohydrate 36g (Dietary Fiber 6g); Protein 2g. **Diet Exchanges:** 1 Vegetable, 2 Fruit.

Orange-Honey Dressing

1/4 cup orange juice

1/4 cup honey

1/2 teaspoon ground cinnamon

Mix all ingredients.

Betty's Special Touch

Arrange this salad on a bed of greens on individual salad plates. Or for a more dramatic effect, use a deep platter and arrange the fruit on top of the greens in alternating bands of color; sprinkle with the jicama stars and cranberries.

Orange-Cranberry-Pecan Salad

Prep: 20 min   **Cook:** 5 min

6 servings

Cranberry Vinaigrette (below)

1/2 cup pecan halves (2 ounces)

2 tablespoons sugar

1 bag (10 ounces) romaine and leaf lettuce salad mix (about 4 cups)

1 can (11 ounces) mandarin orange segments, drained

1/2 cup dried cranberries

1/3 cup thinly sliced red onion

1 Make Cranberry Vinaigrette; set aside.

2 Spray sheet of waxed paper with cooking spray. Heat pecans and sugar in 6-inch nonstick skillet over medium heat about 5 minutes, stirring constantly, until sugar begins to caramelize. Transfer pecans to waxed paper. Let cool; break apart.

3 Toss remaining ingredients and vinaigrette in large bowl. Sprinkle with pecans.

1 Serving: Calories 280 (Calories from Fat 170); Fat 19g (Saturated 2g); Cholesterol 0mg; Sodium 125mg; Carbohydrate 25g (Dietary Fiber 3g); Protein 2g. **Diet Exchanges:** 3 Vegetable, 1 Fruit, 3 Fat.

Cranberry Vinaigrette

1/3 cup olive or vegetable oil

3 tablespoons cranberry-flavored white wine vinegar or regular white wine vinegar

2 tablespoons sugar

1 teaspoon Dijon mustard

1/4 teaspoon salt

Shake all ingredients in tightly covered container.

Betty's Do-Ahead

Prepare the caramelized pecans up to 2 days ahead of time. Store the pecans, covered, at room temperature. Or for a simpler variation, just sprinkle the salad with toasted pecans (page 56).

Delicious Desserts

Blue Ribbon Pies

What could be a more perfect finale to your spectacular Thanksgiving dinner than a home-baked pie, filled with the best of the season? Everyone loves pie, and baking a great pie doesn't have to be hard—once you know the basics.

Making It Easy As Pie

Making pastry is easier than you think. For great recipes, turn to One-Crust Flaky Pastry (page 155) and Two-Crust Flaky Pastry (page 161). Then follow these 3 simple steps.

Step 1. Easy-does-it mixing

- Use a pastry blender to cut shortening into flour. If you don't have one, use two knives and this technique: holding a knife in each hand with blades almost touching, move knives back and forth in opposite directions in a parallel cutting motion. The side of a fork or a wire whisk works, too.

- Mix only until all ingredients are worked in. If you overwork pastry dough, it'll become tough.

- For easier rolling, after you've made the pastry dough and shaped it into a flattened round, wrap it tightly and refrigerate for at least 30 minutes or overnight.

Use a pastry blender to cut shortening into flour

Step 2. Nonstick rolling

- Anchor a pastry cloth or kitchen towel (not terry cloth) around a large cutting board (at least 12 × 12 inches) with masking tape, and use a cloth cover (stockinet) for your rolling pin. Rub flour into both cloths (this will prevent sticking and won't work flour into the pastry). If you don't have a rolling pin cover or pastry cloth, rub flour on the rolling pin and your kitchen table, the countertop or a large cutting board.

- Place pastry dough on a flat surface and start rolling from the center out, lifting and turning pastry occasionally to keep it from sticking. If the pastry begins to stick, rub more flour, a little at a time, on the flat surface and rolling pin.

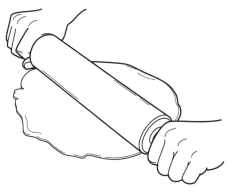

Roll pastry dough from the center out

Step 3. Placing the pastry

- Fold pastry into fourths, and place it in the pie plate with the point in the center of the plate. Unfold and gently ease into plate, being careful not to stretch pastry, which will cause it to shrink when baked.

- Instead of folding pastry, you can roll pastry loosely around rolling pin and transfer to pie plate. Unroll pastry and ease into plate.

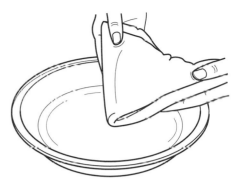

Fold pastry into fourths and place in pie pan

Winning Pie Tips

Even a beginner cook can make a blue-ribbon pie with just a little practice and these expert tips:

- **Pie plates:** Choose a heat-resistant glass pie plate or a dull-finish aluminum pie pan; don't use a shiny pie pan because your pie will have a soggy bottom crust.

- **Pie plate size:** The most common pie size is 9 inches. These recipes were developed with pie plates that hold about 5 cups of ingredients. We sometimes use up to 8 cups of fruit for a two-crust pie to give you a nice, full baked pie, because the fruit does cook down some during baking.

- **Flour:** Use all-purpose flour, or for a more golden color, use unbleached flour. (If using self-rising flour, don't add salt; pastry made with self-rising flour will be slightly different—mealy and tender instead of flaky and tender.)

- **Fat:** It's best to use the fat called for in the recipe; shortening is the type of fat used most often and results in a flaky crust. Pastry and crusts contain enough fat that you don't have to grease pie plates or pans.

continues

Forming Your Crust

The crust you select to make depends on the filling inside. Custard pies are usually baked in one-crust pies; fruit fillings are often cooked in two-crust pies. A juicy fruit pie with a lattice top is more likely to bubble over than a two-crust pie, so be sure to build up a high pastry edge.

One-Crust Pies

• For pies with crusts that are baked together with the filling, such as pumpkin, pecan or custard pie, trim overhanging edge of pastry 1 inch from rim of pie plate. Fold and roll pastry under, even with plate; flute edge.

• For pies with crusts baked completely before filling is added, such as coconut cream or lemon meringue pie, heat oven to 475°; trim overhanging edge of pastry 1 inch from rim of pie plate. Fold and roll pastry under, even with plate; flute edge. Prick bottom and side of pastry thoroughly with fork. Bake 8 to 10 minutes or until light brown; cool on wire rack.

Two-Crust Pies

• For pies with fruit fillings such as apple pie, place bottom crust in pie plate as directed in One-Crust Pies, but do not trim edge. Add desired filling to pastry-lined pie plate. Trim overhanging edge of bottom pastry 1/2 inch from rim of plate. Roll second round of pastry. Fold pastry into fourths and cut slits so steam can escape, or cut slits in pastry and roll pastry loosely around rolling pin. Place top pastry over filling and unfold or unroll. Trim overhanging edge of top pastry 1 inch from rim of plate. Fold and roll top edge under lower edge, pressing on rim to seal; flute edge. Bake as directed in pie recipe.

Lattice Pie Top

For a decorative, finished look to your pie, try a lattice top. Make pastry as directed for Two-Crust Pies, but trim overhanging edge of bottom pastry 1 inch from rim of plate. Roll out pastry for top crust, then cut into 1/2-inch-wide strips. (Use a pastry wheel to cut decorative strips.)

• Place 5 to 7 strips of pastry across filling in pie plate. Weave a cross-strip through center by first folding back every other strip of the first 5 to 7 strips. Continue weaving, folding back alternate strips before adding each cross-strip, until lattice is complete. Trim ends of strips. Fold trimmed edge of bottom crust over ends of strips, building up a high edge. Seal and flute. Bake as directed in recipe.

Classic Lattice Top

Easy Lattice Top

• Place 5 to 7 strips of pastry across filling. Place cross-strips over tops of first strips instead of weaving strips.

Finishing Touch

Fluting the pastry edge makes your pie picture pretty. Choose from:

- **Fork Edge:** Flatten pastry evenly on rim of pie plate. Firmly press tines of fork around edge. To prevent sticking, occasionally dip fork into flour.

- **Pinch Edge:** Place index finger on inside of pastry rim and thumb and index finger (or knuckles) on outside. Pinch pastry into V shape along edge. Pinch again to sharpen points.

- **Rope Edge:** Place side of thumb on pastry rim at an angle. Pinch pastry by pressing the knuckle of your index finger down into pastry toward thumb.

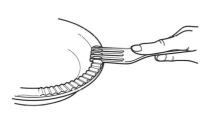 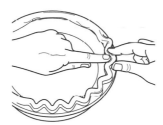 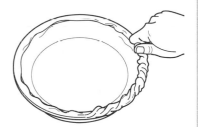

Food Stylists' Secrets

To make your pastry look extra special, follow these easy suggestions. The Betty Crocker Kitchens' food stylists add a little shine before baking by brushing top pastry with:

- **Milk,** then sprinkle with sugar for a *shiny* top crust.
- **Water,** then sprinkle with sugar for a *sugary* crust.
- **Beaten egg yolk** mixed with 1 teaspoon milk for a *golden* crust.

continues

Baking Your Pies and Pastry

Pies are baked at high temperatures (375° to 425°) so the rich pastry becomes flaky and golden brown and the filling cooks all the way through. Follow your recipe to determine the exact bake time.

Pastry Preventions

You've heard the saying "an ounce of prevention is worth a pound of cure." The same is true of pies. Here are a few prevention tips to give you the best-looking and best-tasting pies.

Prevent edges from overbrowning

- **Pastry Overbrowning:** To prevent pie crust and pastry edges from getting too brown, cover them with a strip of aluminum foil, gently molding foil to edge of pie. Or tear off a piece of aluminum foil 1 inch larger than the pie plate. Fold sheet of foil into fourths; cut out center, leaving about a 2-inch rim for around the outside of the pie. Bake pie as directed, removing the foil 15 minutes before end of bake time so the edge can brown.

- **Soggy Pie Crust:** To prevent a one-crust pie crust and pastry edges from becoming soggy, partially bake pastry before adding filling. Heat oven to 425°. Carefully place a double-thickness sheet of aluminum foil on bottom pastry, gently pressing foil to bottom and side of pastry. Let foil extend over edge to prevent excessive browning. Bake 10 minutes; carefully remove foil and bake 2 to 4 minutes longer or until pastry just begins to brown and has become set. If crust bubbles, gently push bubbles down with back of spoon. Fill and bake as directed in pie recipe, adjusting oven temperature if necessary.

- **Puffed-Up Pastry:** To prevent an unfilled one-crust pie crust from puffing up as it bakes, prick the pastry thoroughly with a fork before baking to allow steam to escape. (For one-crust pies where the filling is baked in the crust, such as pumpkin or pecan pie, *don't* prick the crust because the filling will seep under the crust during baking.) Nonstick pie pans can cause an unfilled one-crust pie crust to shrink excessively during baking. To hold the pastry in place, hook it over the edge of the pan and prick it with a fork before baking.

Serving and Storing Your Pies

Most of the pies in this cookbook make 8 servings. If a pie is really rich, it makes 10 to 12 servings.

- An easy way to cut a pie into an even number of pieces is to cut the pie in half, then into fourths, and then cut each fourth in half before removing a slice.

- Store pies that contain eggs, such as pumpkin and cream pies, in the refrigerator.

- You can freeze both unbaked and baked pie crusts. Unbaked crusts will keep for 2 months in the freezer; baked crusts for 4 months. To prevent soggy bottoms, don't thaw *unbaked* crusts; bake them right after taking them out of the freezer. To thaw *baked* pie crusts, unwrap and let stand at room temperature, or heat in the oven at 350° for about 6 minutes.

- Tuck away a treat for later—freeze a whole fruit pie! For best results, the pie should be baked and cooled completely first. Then put it in the freezer uncovered. When it's completely frozen, wrap the pie tightly or put it in a plastic freezer bag and pop it back in the freezer. Frozen baked fruit pies will keep up to 4 months. (Do not freeze custard or cream pies.)

Pastry Rx

What if my pastry is:	Possible Cause
Too pale in color	• Baked in shiny pan • Underbaked
Looks smooth	• Pastry was handled too much
Bottom crust is soggy	• Baked in shiny pan • Oven temperature too low
Tough	• Too much water • Too much flour • Pastry mixed and handled too much
Too tender; falls apart	• Too little water • Too much shortening
Dry and mealy, not flaky	• Shortening cut in too finely • Too little water

Classic Pumpkin Pie

Prep: 25 min   **Bake:** 1 hr   **Cool:** 30 min   **Chill:** 4 hr   **Stand:** 5 min   **8 servings**

One-Crust Flaky Pastry (below)

2 eggs

1/2 cup sugar

1 teaspoon ground cinnamon

1/2 teaspoon salt

1/2 teaspoon ground ginger

1/8 teaspoon ground cloves

1 can (15 ounces) pumpkin (not pumpkin pie mix)

1 can (12 ounces) evaporated milk

Spiced Cream Clouds (below)

1 Heat oven to 425°. Make One-Crust Flaky Pastry.

2 Beat eggs slightly in medium bowl with wire whisk or hand beater. Beat in remaining ingredients except Spiced Cream Clouds.

3 Place pastry-lined pie plate on oven rack to prevent spilling the filling. Pour filling into pie plate. Cover edge with 2- to 3-inch strip of aluminum foil to prevent excessive browning; remove foil during last 15 minutes of baking. Bake 15 minutes.

4 Reduce oven temperature to 350°. Bake about 45 minutes longer or until knife inserted in center comes out clean. Cool 30 minutes. Refrigerate about 4 hours or until chilled. Make Spiced Cream Clouds.

5 Top slices of pie with frozen Spiced Cream Clouds; let stand 5 minutes before serving. Store pie covered in refrigerator.

1 Serving: Calories 340 (Calories from Fat 170); Fat 18g (Saturated 7g); Cholesterol 75mg; Sodium 300mg; Carbohydrate 36g (Dietary Fiber 2g); Protein 8g. **Diet Exchanges:** Not Recommended.

All About Fresh Pumpkin

 Q. **I have fresh pumpkin from my garden (or the farmers' market)—how can I use it?**

A. Here's a fresh alternative to canned pumpkin. Heat oven to 350°. Cut 2-pound sugar pumpkin crosswise in half; scrape out seeds and fibers. Place cut side down in large shallow baking pan. Bake uncovered 50 to 70 minutes or until tender when pierced through skin with a fork; cool. Scoop pulp from skins. Puree pulp in food processor or blender, pulsing on and off, until smooth; or mash thoroughly with a potato masher. Place pumpkin puree in a strainer and allow to drain at least 30 minutes (to become as thick as canned pumpkin). Refrigerate or freeze any remaining puree.

One-Crust Flaky Pastry

1 cup all-purpose flour

1/4 teaspoon salt

1/3 cup plus 1 tablespoon shortening

2 to 3 tablespoons cold water

Mix flour and salt in medium bowl. Cut in shortening, using pastry blender or crisscrossing 2 knives, until particles are size of small peas. Sprinkle with cold water, 1 tablespoon at a time, tossing with fork until all flour is moistened and pastry almost leaves side of bowl (1 to 2 teaspoons more water can be added if necessary). Gather pastry into a ball. Shape into flattened round on lightly floured surface. Roll pastry, using floured rolling pin, into circle 2 inches larger than upside-down pie plate, 9 × 1 1/4 inches. Fold pastry into fourths; place in pie plate. Unfold and ease into plate, pressing firmly against bottom and side. Trim overhanging edge of pastry 1 inch from rim of pie plate. Fold and roll pastry under, even with plate; flute as desired.

Spiced Cream Clouds

1/2 cup whipping (heavy) cream

1 tablespoon packed brown sugar

1/4 teaspoon pumpkin pie spice or ground cinnamon

Beat all ingredients in chilled small bowl with electric mixer on high speed until stiff. Place waxed paper on cookie sheet. Drop whipped cream by 8 spoonfuls onto waxed paper. Freeze uncovered at least 2 hours. Place in freezer container; cover tightly and freeze no longer than 2 months.

Betty's Special Touch

You can decorate your pies with pretty pastry shapes cut from leftover unbaked pastry. Cut the pastry into shapes with a leaf-shaped or other cookie cutter, sprinkle with a little granulated sugar and cinnamon and bake on an ungreased cookie sheet at 425° for 8 to 10 minutes or until lightly browned.

No-Crust Harvest Pumpkin Pie

Prep: 20 min   **Bake:** 55 min   **Cool:** 15 min   **Chill:** 4 hr   **8 servings**

Brown Sugar Topping (below)

1 can (15 ounces) pumpkin (not pumpkin pie mix)

1 can (12 ounces) evaporated fat-free milk

3 egg whites or 1/2 cup fat-free cholesterol-free egg product

1/2 cup sugar

1/2 cup all-purpose flour

1 1/2 teaspoons pumpkin pie spice

3/4 teaspoon baking powder

1/8 teaspoon salt

2 teaspoons grated orange peel

1 Heat oven to 350°. Spray pie plate, 10 × 1 1/2 inches, with cooking spray. Make Brown Sugar Topping; set aside.

2 Place remaining ingredients in blender or food processor in order listed. Cover and blend on medium-high speed until smooth. Place pie plate on oven rack to prevent spilling the filling. Pour filling into pie plate. Sprinkle with topping.

3 Bake 50 to 55 minutes or until knife inserted in center comes out clean. Cool 15 minutes. Refrigerate about 4 hours or until chilled. Store pie covered in refrigerator.

1 Serving: Calories 185 (Calories from Fat 20); Fat 2g (Saturated 1g); Cholesterol 5mg; Sodium 170mg; Carbohydrate 37g (Dietary Fiber 2g); Protein 7g. **Diet Exchanges:** 2 Starch, 1 Vegetable.

Brown Sugar Topping

1/4 cup packed brown sugar

1/4 cup quick-cooking oats

1 tablespoon butter or margarine, softened

Mix all ingredients.

Betty's Helpful Tip

Put away that rolling pin! Whip this lighter pumpkin pie together in a blender or food processor, and pour it directly into the pie plate. It's easy and delicious! Glass pie plates work best for this recipe.

Impossibly Easy Pumpkin Pie

Prep: 7 min   **Bake:** 40 min   **Cool:** 2 hr   **8 servings**

1 cup canned pumpkin (not pumpkin pie mix)

1/2 cup Original or Reduced Fat Bisquick® mix

1/2 cup sugar

1 cup evaporated milk

1 tablespoon butter or margarine, softened

1 1/2 teaspoons pumpkin pie spice

1 teaspoon vanilla

2 eggs

Sweetened whipped cream, if desired

1 Heat oven to 350°. Grease pie plate, 9 × 1 1/4 inches, with shortening.

2 Mix all ingredients except whipped cream with fork until blended. Place pie plate on oven rack to prevent spilling the filling. Pour filling into pie plate.

3 Bake 35 to 40 minutes or until knife inserted in center comes out clean. Cool 2 hours. Serve with whipped cream. Store pie covered in refrigerator.

1 Serving: Calories 155 (Calories from Fat 45); Fat 5g (Saturated 2g); Cholesterol 60mg; Sodium 170mg; Carbohydrate 23g (Dietary Fiber 1g); Protein 5g. **Diet Exchanges:** 1 Starch, 1 Vegetable, 1 Fat.

Betty's Simple Substitution

Pumpkin pie spice is a combination of cinnamon, nutmeg, cloves and ginger. If you don't keep pumpkin pie spice on hand, use 1 teaspoon ground cinnamon, 1/4 teaspoon ground nutmeg, 1/4 teaspoon ground cloves and 1/4 teaspoon ground ginger.

All About
Pumpkin Seeds

Q. **What's the best way to make pumpkin seeds into a snack?**

A. Roasting pumpkin seeds is easy and the whole family can help make this tasty fall treat. It also works well with squash seeds. Here's how:

1 Cut a fresh, well-ripened pumpkin in half. Remove membrane and seeds. Remove most of the pulp from the seeds (leaving some pulp on is okay because it adds to the flavor; for the same reason, do not rinse seeds).

2 Heat oven to 300°. Spread 1 tablespoon vegetable oil in a shallow pan. Sprinkle seeds over oil in single layer. Sprinkle 1 teaspoon salt over seeds.

3 Bake 15 to 20 minutes or until lightly browned; cool. Enjoy!

Pumpkin Cheesecake

Prep: 15 min   **Bake:** 1 hr 40 min   **Stand:** 30 min   **Cool:** 2 hr   **Chill:** 8 hr   **16 servings**

Graham Cracker Crust (below)

1/4 cup all-purpose flour

2 teaspoons pumpkin pie spice

2 tablespoons brandy, if desired

1 can (15 ounces) pumpkin (not pumpkin pie mix)

4 packages (8 ounces each) cream cheese, softened

1 cup packed brown sugar

2/3 cup granulated sugar

5 eggs

1 Heat oven to 350°. Make Graham Cracker Crust. Mix flour, pumpkin pie spice, brandy and pumpkin in small bowl; set aside.

2 Beat cream cheese in large bowl with electric mixer on medium speed until smooth and creamy. Gradually beat in sugars until smooth. Add eggs, one at a time, on low speed, beating just until blended. Gradually beat in pumpkin mixture until smooth. Pour over partially baked crust.

3 Bake 1 hour 20 minutes to 1 hour 30 minutes or until center is set. Turn oven off; open oven door at least 4 inches. Let cheesecake remain in oven 30 minutes. Loosen cheesecake from side of pan, using sharp knife. Cool completely in pan on wire rack, about 2 hours. Refrigerate at least 8 hours or overnight.

4 Carefully remove side of pan before cutting cheesecake. Store cheesecake covered in refrigerator.

1 Serving: Calories 425 (Calories from Fat 260); Fat 29g (Saturated 17g); Cholesterol 145mg; Sodium 290mg; Carbohydrate 34g (Dietary Fiber 1g); Protein 7g. **Diet Exchanges:** Not Recommended.

Graham Cracker Crust

1 tablespoon butter or margarine, softened

1 3/4 cups graham cracker crumbs (about 24 squares)

2 tablespoons sugar

1/2 cup butter or margarine, melted

Grease bottom and side of springform pan, 9 × 3 inches, with 1 tablespoon butter. Mix cracker crumbs, sugar and 1/2 cup butter. Press in bottom of pan. Bake 8 to 10 minutes or until set. Cool 5 minutes at room temperature. Refrigerate about 5 minutes or until completely cooled.

Betty's Helpful Tip

To help prevent cracks in the cheesecake, don't overbeat the mixture once the eggs are added. Be sure to let the cheesecake stand in the oven for the full 30 minutes after baking, as directed in the recipe.

Sweet Potato Pie

Prep: 15 min   **Bake:** 1 hr 5 min   **Cool:** 30 min   **Chill:** 4 hr   **8 servings**

Pat-in-the-Pan Pastry
(below) or One-Crust
Flaky Pastry (page 155)

2 eggs

3/4 cup sugar

1 teaspoon ground
cinnamon

1/2 teaspoon salt

1/2 teaspoon
ground ginger

1/4 teaspoon
ground cloves

1 can (23 ounces) sweet
potatoes, drained and
mashed (1 3/4 to 2 cups)

1 can (12 ounces)
evaporated milk

Sweetened whipped
cream, if desired

1 Heat oven to 425°. Make Pat-in-the-Pan Pastry.

2 Beat eggs slightly in medium bowl with hand beater. Beat in remaining ingredients except whipped cream.

3 Place pastry-lined pie plate on oven rack to prevent spilling the filling. Pour filling into pie plate. (If using One-Crust Flaky Pastry, cover edge with 2- to 3-inch strip of aluminum foil to prevent excessive browning.) Bake 15 minutes.

4 Reduce oven temperature to 350°. Bake 45 to 50 minutes longer or until knife inserted in center comes out clean. (Remove foil strip, if using, during last 15 minutes of baking.) Cool at room temperature 30 minutes. Refrigerate at least 4 hours until chilled. Serve with whipped cream. Store pie covered in refrigerator.

1 **Serving:** Calories 385 (Calories from Fat 125); Fat 14g (Saturated 4g); Cholesterol 60mg; Sodium 320mg; Carbohydrate 57g (Dietary Fiber 3g); Protein 8g. **Diet Exchanges:** Not Recommended.

Pat-in-the-Pan Pastry

1 1/3 cups all-purpose
flour

1/3 cup vegetable oil

1/2 teaspoon salt

2 tablespoons cold water

Mix flour, oil and salt with a fork in medium bowl until all flour is moistened. Sprinkle with cold water, 1 tablespoon at a time, tossing with fork until all water is absorbed. Shape pastry into a ball, using your hands. Press pastry in bottom and up side of pie plate or pie pan.

Praline Sweet Potato Pie: Decrease second bake time to 35 minutes. Mix 1/3 cup packed brown sugar, 1/3 cup chopped pecans and 1 tablespoon butter or margarine, softened; sprinkle over pie. Bake about 10 minutes longer or until knife inserted in center comes out clean.

Betty's Special Touch

If you're making your first pie and you don't want to tackle rolling out pie dough, try this really easy pastry that you simply pat and press into the pan—no rolling pin required! It can be used in any recipe that calls for One-Crust Flaky Pastry.

Nutty Squash Pie

Prep: 15 min   **Bake:** 1 hr 10 min   **Cool:** 2 hr   **8 servings**

(see photo insert)

Nut Cookie Crust (below)

2 eggs

1 cup cooled mashed cooked squash, sweet potatoes or pumpkin

3/4 cup packed brown sugar

1 teaspoon ground cinnamon

1/2 teaspoon salt

1/4 teaspoon ground cloves

1/4 teaspoon ground ginger

1/4 teaspoon ground nutmeg

1 can (12 ounces) evaporated milk

1 Heat oven to 425°. Make Nut Cookie Crust.

2 Beat eggs slightly in large bowl. Stir in remaining ingredients except milk until smooth. Gradually stir in milk. Pour into crust. Cover edge with 2- to 3-inch strip of aluminum foil to prevent excessive browning; remove foil during last 15 minutes of baking. Bake 15 minutes.

3 Reduce oven temperature to 350°. Bake 45 to 55 minutes longer or until knife inserted near center comes out clean. Cool completely on wire rack, about 2 hours. Store covered in refrigerator.

1 **Serving:** Calories 425 (Calories from Fat 180); Fat 20g (Saturated 9g); Cholesterol 90mg; Sodium 420mg; Carbohydrate 53g (Dietary Fiber 2g); Protein 8g. **Diet Exchanges:** Not Recommended.

Nut Cookie Crust

1/2 cup butter or margarine, softened

1/3 cup packed brown sugar

1 1/4 cups all-purpose flour

1/2 cup chopped nuts

1/2 teaspoon vanilla

1/4 teaspoon salt

1/4 teaspoon baking soda

Mix butter and brown sugar in large bowl. Stir in remaining ingredients just until crumbly. Press crust mixture on bottom and side of ungreased deep-dish pie plate, 9 × 1 1/2 inches, or regular pie plate, 9 × 1 1/4 inches, building up 1/2-inch edge (high edge is necessary to prevent filling from running over).

Betty's Special Touch

Crown this tasty pie with Brown Sugar Whipped Cream. To make, beat 1 cup whipping (heavy) cream and 3 tablespoons packed brown sugar in chilled small bowl with electric mixer on high speed until stiff.

Classic Apple Pie

Prep: 45 min   **Bake:** 50 min   **Cool:** 2 hr   **8 servings**

Two-Crust Flaky Pastry (below)

1/3 to 2/3 cup sugar

1/4 cup all-purpose flour

1/2 teaspoon ground cinnamon

1/2 teaspoon ground nutmeg

Dash of salt

8 cups thinly sliced peeled tart apples (8 medium)

2 tablespoons butter or margarine, if desired

1 Heat oven to 425°. Make Two-Crust Flaky Pastry.

2 Mix sugar, flour, cinnamon, nutmeg and salt in large bowl. Stir in apples. Place apple mixture in pastry-lined pie plate. Cut butter into small pieces; sprinkle over apples.

3 Roll other round of pastry; fold into fourths and cut slits so steam can escape. Place pastry over apples and unfold. Trim overhanging edge of top pastry 1 inch from rim of pie plate. Fold and roll top edge under lower edge, pressing on rim to seal; flute as desired. Cover edge with 2- to 3-inch strip of aluminum foil to prevent excessive browning; remove foil during last 15 minutes of baking.

4 Bake 40 to 50 minutes or until crust is golden brown and juice begins to bubble through slits in crust. Cool on wire rack at least 2 hours.

1 Serving: Calories 400 (Calories from Fat 180); Fat 20g (Saturated 3g); Cholesterol 0mg; Sodium 300mg; Carbohydrate 52g (Dietary Fiber 2g); Protein 5g. **Diet Exchanges:** Not Recommended.

Two-Crust Flaky Pastry

2 cups all-purpose flour

1 teaspoon salt

2/3 cup plus 2 tablespoons shortening

4 to 5 tablespoons cold water

Mix flour and salt in medium bowl. Cut in shortening, using pastry blender or crisscrossing 2 knives, until particles are size of small peas. Sprinkle with cold water, 1 tablespoon at a time, tossing with fork until all flour is moistened and pastry almost leaves side of bowl (1 to 2 teaspoons more water can be added if necessary). Gather pastry into a ball. Divide pastry in half. Shape each half into flattened round on lightly floured surface. Roll 1 round of pastry, using floured rolling pin, into circle 2 inches larger than upside-down pie plate, 9 × 1 1/4 inches. Fold pastry into fourths; place in pie plate. Unfold and ease into plate, pressing firmly against bottom and side. Trim overhanging edge of pastry 1/2 inch from rim of pie plate.

Betty's Helpful Tip

Apple varieties great for this pie include Granny Smith, Jonagold and Rome.

French Apple Pie: Heat oven to 425°. Make One-Crust Flaky Pastry (page 155). Place apple mixture (from Classic Apple Pie) in pastry-lined pie plate; omit butter. Make crumb topping: Mix 1 cup all-purpose flour, 1/2 cup packed brown sugar and 1/2 cup firm butter or margarine until crumbly; sprinkle over apples. Cover topping with aluminum foil during last 10 minutes of baking to prevent excessive browning. Bake pie 50 minutes. Serve warm.

Apple Wrapper Pie

Prep: 40 min   **Bake:** 35 min   **Cool:** 1 hr   **8 servings**

One-Crust Flaky Pastry (page 155)

2/3 cup packed brown sugar

1/3 cup all-purpose flour

4 cups thinly sliced peeled tart apples (4 medium)

1 tablespoon butter or stick margarine

Granulated sugar, if desired

1 Heat oven to 425°. Make One-Crust Flaky Pastry—except roll pastry into 13-inch circle on lightly floured surface. Place on large ungreased cookie sheet. Cover with plastic wrap to keep moist while making filling.

2 Mix brown sugar and flour in large bowl. Stir in apples. Mound apple mixture on center of pastry to within 3 inches of edge. Cut butter into small pieces; sprinkle over apples. Fold edge of pastry over apples, making pleats so it lays flat on apples. Sprinkle pastry with sugar.

3 Bake 30 to 35 minutes or until crust is light golden brown. To prevent excessive browning, cover center of pie with 5-inch square of aluminum foil during last 10 to 15 minutes of baking. Cool on cookie sheet on wire rack 1 hour, or serve warm if desired.

1 Serving: Calories 285 (Calories from Fat 110); Fat 12g (Saturated 4g); Cholesterol 5mg; Sodium 165mg; Carbohydrate 42g (Dietary Fiber 1g); Protein 3g. **Diet Exchanges:** 1 Starch, 2 Fruit, 2 Fat.

Apple-Mince Streusel Pie: Heat oven to 425°. Make One-Crust Flaky Pastry (page 155). Mix 3 cups thinly sliced peeled eating apples (3 medium), 3 tablespoons all-purpose flour and 2 tablespoons butter or margarine, melted; place apple mixture in pastry-lined pie plate. Spoon 1 jar (27 ounces) prepared mincemeat (3 cups) over apples. To make streusel, mix 1/2 cup all-purpose flour, 1/4 cup packed brown sugar and 1 teaspoon ground cinnamon in medium bowl. Cut in 1/3 cup cold butter or margarine, using pastry blender or crisscrossing 2 knives, until crumbly. Stir in 1/4 cup chopped nuts. Sprinkle over mincemeat. Cover edge of pastry with 2- to 3-inch strip of aluminum foil to prevent excessive browning; remove foil during last 15 minutes of baking. Bake 10 minutes. Reduce oven temperature to 375°. Bake 25 to 30 minutes longer or until crust is golden brown. Cool on wire rack at least 2 hours.

Pear-Raisin Pie

Prep: 25 min   **Cook:** 10 min   **Bake:** 30 min   **8 servings**

Streusel Topping (below)

1 cup Original Bisquick mix

1/4 cup butter or margarine, softened

2 tablespoons boiling water

1/2 cup pineapple juice

1/2 cup raisins

1 tablespoon cornstarch

1/8 teaspoon ground nutmeg

1/8 teaspoon ground ginger

4 cups sliced peeled pears (about 3 medium)

1 Heat oven to 375°. Make Streusel Topping; set aside. Stir together Bisquick mix and butter in medium bowl. Add boiling water; stir vigorously until very soft dough forms. Press dough firmly in ungreased pie plate, 9 × 1 1/4 inches, using hands dusted with Bisquick mix, bringing dough onto rim of pie plate. Flute if desired.

2 Mix pineapple juice, raisins, cornstarch, nutmeg and ginger in 2-quart saucepan. Cook over medium heat, stirring constantly, until mixture thickens and boils. Boil and stir 1 minute; remove from heat. Stir in pears. Spoon into pie plate. Sprinkle with topping.

3 Bake 25 to 30 minutes or until crust and topping are light golden brown.

1 Serving: Calories 325 (Calories from Fat 135); Fat 15g (Saturated 8g); Cholesterol 30mg; Sodium 400mg; Carbohydrate 45g (Dietary Fiber 3g); Protein 3g. **Diet Exchanges:** Not recommended.

Streusel Topping

2/3 cup quick-cooking oats

1/2 cup Original Bisquick mix

1/3 cup packed brown sugar

1/4 cup firm butter or margarine

Mix oats, Bisquick mix and brown sugar. Cut in butter, using fork or pastry blender, until mixture is crumbly.

Betty's Helpful Tip

Pears rock hard? To speed up the ripening process, place them in a paper bag with an apple. Pierce the bag in several places with the tip of a knife, and leave at room temperature. Serve this streusel-topped pie warm topped with slices of Cheddar cheese cut into maple leaf shapes with a cookie cutter.

Orchard Squares

Prep: 20 min   **Bake:** 40 min   **15 servings**

**Toasted Almond Pastry
(below)**

**1/3 to 2/3 cup granulated
sugar**

1/3 cup all-purpose flour

**1/2 teaspoon
ground nutmeg**

Dash of salt

**3 cups frozen sliced
peaches, thawed and
drained**

**3 cups sliced fresh pears
(3 medium)**

**2 cups thinly sliced
peeled tart cooking
apples (2 medium)**

**2 tablespoons lemon
juice**

**2 tablespoons butter
or margarine**

3/4 cup powdered sugar

About 1 tablespoon milk

Ice cream, if desired

1 Heat oven to 425°. Make Toasted Almond Pastry. Gather pastry into a ball; cut in half. Shape each half into flattened round on lightly floured cloth-covered surface. Roll 1 round into 18 × 13-inch rectangle with floured cloth-covered rolling pin. Fold pastry into fourths; unfold and ease into ungreased jelly roll pan, 15 1/2 × 10 1/2 × 1 inch. Trim overhanging edge of pastry 1/2 inch from rim of pan.

2 Mix granulated sugar, flour, nutmeg and salt in large bowl. Stir in peaches, pears and apples. Place fruit mixture in pastry-lined pan. Drizzle with lemon juice. Cut butter into small pieces; sprinkle over fruit mixture. Roll other round of pastry into 17 × 12-inch rectangle. Fold into fourths; place over filling and unfold. Trim overhanging edge of top pastry 1 inch from rim of pan. Fold and roll top edge under lower edge, pressing on rim to seal; flute as desired (see Finishing Touch, page 151); cut slits so steam can escape. Cover edge with 2- to 3-inch strip of aluminum foil to prevent excessive browning; remove foil during last 15 minutes of baking.

3 Bake 35 to 40 minutes or until crust is golden brown and juice begins to bubble through slits in crust; cool slightly. Mix powdered sugar and milk until smooth; drizzle over crust. Cut into about 3-inch squares. Serve warm or cold with ice cream.

1 Serving: Calories 380 (Calories from Fat 180); Fat 20g (Saturated 5g); Cholesterol 5mg; Sodium 170mg; Carbohydrate 46g (Dietary Fiber 3g); Protein 4g. **Diet Exchanges:** Not Recommended.

Toasted Almond Pastry

**3 tablespoons slivered
almonds**

**3 1/2 cups all-purpose
flour**

1 teaspoon salt

1 1/4 cups shortening

**8 to 9 tablespoons
cold water**

Heat oven to 325°. Bake almonds on ungreased cookie sheet 4 to 7 minutes or until lightly browned. Place almonds in food processor or blender. Cover and process until almonds are finely ground. Mix flour, ground almonds and salt in large bowl. Cut in shortening, using pastry blender or crisscrossing 2 knives, until particles are size of small peas. Sprinkle with cold water, 1 tablespoon at a time, tossing with fork until all flour is moistened and pastry almost leaves side of bowl (1 to 2 teaspoons more water can be added if necessary).

Betty's Do-Ahead

This pie is a great choice for a crowd since it's so easy to cut into even-sized square portions (you'll get 15 servings).

Kentucky Pecan Pie

Prep: 15 min   **Bake:** 50 min   **Chill:** 2 hr   **8 servings**

Buttermilk Pastry
(below) or One-Crust
Flaky Pastry (page 155)

2/3 cup sugar

1/3 cup butter or
margarine, melted

1 cup corn syrup

2 tablespoons bourbon,
if desired

1/2 teaspoon salt

3 eggs

1 cup pecan halves
or broken pecans

1 package (6 ounces)
semisweet chocolate
chips (1 cup)

1 Heat oven to 375°. Make Buttermilk Pastry.

2 Beat sugar, butter, corn syrup, bourbon, salt and eggs in large bowl with hand beater. Stir in pecans and chocolate chips. Pour into pastry-lined pie plate. Cover edge with 2- to 3-inch strip of aluminum foil to prevent excessive browning; remove foil during last 15 minutes of baking.

3 Bake 40 to 50 minutes or until set. Refrigerate at least 2 hours until chilled. Store covered in refrigerator.

1 Serving: Calories 625 (Calories from Fat 315); Fat 35g (Saturated 13g); Cholesterol 100mg; Sodium 420mg; Carbohydrate 75g (Dietary Fiber 3g); Protein 6g. **Diet Exchanges:** Not Recommended.

Buttermilk Pastry

2 cups all-purpose flour

1 teaspoon salt

2/3 cup shortening

3 tablespoons butter or
stick margarine

2 teaspoons vegetable oil

1/3 cup buttermilk

Mix flour and salt in medium bowl. Cut in shortening and butter, using pastry blender or crisscrossing 2 knives, until particles are size of small peas. Mix in oil and buttermilk with fork until all flour is moistened and pastry leaves side of bowl. Divide in half; shape each half into a ball. Shape one ball into flattened round on lightly floured surface. Roll pastry, using floured rolling pin, into circle 2 inches larger than upside-down pie plate, 9 × 1 1/4 inches. Fold pastry into fourths; place in pie plate. Unfold and ease into plate, pressing firmly against bottom and side. Trim overhanging edge of pastry 1 inch from rim of pie plate. Fold and roll pastry under, even with plate; flute as desired. Wrap second ball of pastry and freeze for later use.

Pecan Pie: Omit bourbon and chocolate chips.

Brandy Pecan Pie: Decrease corn syrup to 3/4 cup, substitute 1/4 cup brandy for the bourbon and omit chocolate chips.

*Betty's
Helpful Tip*

This extra flaky dough is so easy to roll out and handle. This recipe makes enough for 2 pies, so you can use half and freeze the rest for another pie another day!

Pear-Cranberry Crisp

Prep: 25 min   **Bake:** 40 min   **Cool:** 30 min   **12 servings**

5 cups sliced peeled
pears (5 medium)

1 1/2 cups fresh or
frozen cranberries

1 cup granulated sugar

2 tablespoons all-purpose
flour

2 teaspoons grated
orange peel

1 cup old-fashioned oats

1/2 cup packed brown
sugar

1/3 cup all-purpose flour

1/4 cup butter or
margarine

1/2 cup chopped nuts

Whipped cream,
if desired

1 Heat oven to 375°. Spray rectangular baking dish, 12 × 8 inches
(2-quart size), with cooking spray. Place pears, cranberries, granulated
sugar, 2 tablespoons flour and the orange peel in large bowl; toss to coat.
Spoon into baking dish.

2 Mix oats, brown sugar and 1/3 cup flour in small bowl. Cut in butter,
using fork or pastry blender, until mixture is crumbly. Stir in nuts.
Sprinkle evenly over fruit mixture.

3 Bake 30 to 40 minutes or until topping is golden brown and fruit is
tender. Cool 30 minutes. Serve warm with whipped cream.

1 Serving: Calories 280 (Calories from Fat 810); Fat 9g (Saturated 2g); Cholesterol 5mg; Sodium 50mg;
Carbohydrate 47g (Dietary Fiber 3g); Protein 3g. **Diet Exchanges:** 1 Starch, 2 Fruit, 2 Fat.

Betty's Simple Substitution

This tasty crisp is good
with any fall fruit; apples
are a good substitute for
the pears. Or make it a
triple treat by using a
combination of apples,
pears and cranberries.

Cranberry-Raspberry Bread Pudding

Prep: 5 min   **Bake:** 55 min

(see photo insert)

1 loaf (8 ounces) French bread

3 eggs

1/3 cup granulated sugar

1/2 teaspoon ground cinnamon

Dash of salt

1 1/2 cups milk

2 tablespoons packed brown sugar

Cran-Raspberry Topping (below)

1 Heat oven to 325°. Grease bottom and sides of square pan, 8 × 8 × 2 or 9 × 9 × 2 inches, with shortening.

2 Tear bread into 1-inch pieces to equal about 8 cups. Spread bread pieces evenly in pan.

3 Beat eggs, granulated sugar, cinnamon and salt in medium bowl with fork or wire whisk until blended. Beat in milk. Pour over bread in pan. Sprinkle with brown sugar.

4 Bake uncovered 50 to 55 minutes or until golden brown. While bread pudding is baking, make Cran-Raspberry Topping. Serve warm bread pudding with topping.

1 Serving: Calories 290 (Calories from Fat 35); Fat 4g (Saturated 1g); Cholesterol 75mg; Sodium 220mg; Carbohydrate 57g (Dietary Fiber 3g); Protein 6g. **Diet Exchanges:** 2 Starch, 2 Fruit.

Cran-Raspberry Topping

1 package (10 ounces) frozen raspberries in syrup, thawed

1 cup granulated sugar

1 cup fresh or frozen (thawed) cranberries

Drain raspberries in strainer, reserving 1/2 cup syrup. Mix syrup and sugar in 2 quart saucepan. Cook over medium heat, stirring constantly, until mixture thickens and boils. Continue boiling 1 to 2 minutes, stirring constantly. Stir in raspberries and cranberries. Reduce heat just enough so mixture bubbles gently. Cook about 3 minutes, stirring occasionally, until cranberries are tender but do not burst.

Betty's Helpful Tip

For 10 servings, double all ingredients in the recipe except the French bread. Bake in a greased 13 × 9-inch rectangular pan. There's no need to double the Cran-Raspberry Topping.

Sweet Maple Maize Pudding

Prep: 30 min   **Bake:** 1 hr 30 min   **Cool:** 2 hr   **8 servings**

1/2 cup maple-flavored
syrup

1 teaspoon ground
cinnamon

1/2 teaspoon
ground ginger

1/4 teaspoon salt

1/4 teaspoon
ground nutmeg

4 cups milk

1/2 cup yellow cornmeal

1/2 cup full-flavor or
mild-flavor molasses

2 tablespoons butter
or margarine

2 eggs, beaten

Whipped cream,
if desired

1 Heat oven to 350°. Spray 2-quart casserole with cooking spray. Mix maple syrup, cinnamon, ginger, salt and nutmeg until well blended; set aside.

2 Heat milk in 3-quart saucepan over medium heat just until tiny bubbles form at the edge (do not boil); stir in cornmeal. Cook over medium-low heat about 20 minutes, stirring constantly, until very thick; remove from heat. Stir in maple syrup mixture and remaining ingredients except whipped cream.

3 Pour into casserole. Place casserole in rectangular pan, 13 × 9 × 2 inches, on oven rack. Pour boiling water into pan until 1 inch deep. Bake 1 hour 20 minutes to 1 hour 30 minutes or until knife inserted halfway to center comes out clean. Cool about 2 hours. Serve with whipped cream.

1 Serving: Calories 225 (Calories from Fat 65); Fat 7g (Saturated 4g); Cholesterol 70mg; Sodium 180mg; Carbohydrate 34g (Dietary Fiber 1g); Protein 6g. **Diet Exchanges:** 1 Starch, 1 Fruit, 1/2 Milk, 1 Fat.

Betty's Do-Ahead

You can make this Native American cornmeal pudding ahead of time and store it in the refrigerator. Serve cold, or to reheat, place individual servings on small plates and heat uncovered in the microwave on Medium for 30 to 40 seconds or until warm.

Apple Pudding Cake
with Cinnamon Butter Sauce

Prep: 15 min   **Bake:** 35 min   **9 servings**

1 cup packed brown sugar

1/4 cup butter or margarine, softened

1 egg

1 cup all-purpose flour

1 teaspoon baking soda

1 teaspoon ground cinnamon

1/2 teaspoon ground nutmeg

1/4 teaspoon salt

2 cups chopped peeled or unpeeled cooking apples (2 medium)

Cinnamon Butter Sauce (below)

1 Heat oven to 350°. Grease bottom and sides of square pan, 8 × 8 × 2 inches, with shortening.

2 Mix brown sugar and butter in large bowl with spoon until light and fluffy. Beat in egg. Stir in flour, baking soda, cinnamon, nutmeg and salt. Stir in apples. Spread batter in pan.

3 Bake 25 to 35 minutes or until toothpick inserted in center comes out clean. While cake is baking, make Cinnamon Butter Sauce. Serve warm sauce over warm cake.

1 Serving: Calories 340 (Calories from Fat 125); Fat 14g (Saturated 8g); Cholesterol 60mg; Sodium 310mg; Carbohydrate 54g (Dietary Fiber 1g); Protein 3g. **Diet Exchanges:** Not Recommended.

Cinnamon Butter Sauce

1/3 cup butter or margarine

2/3 cup sugar

1/3 cup half-and-half

1/2 teaspoon ground cinnamon

Heat all ingredients in 1-quart saucepan over medium heat, stirring frequently, until butter is melted and sauce is hot.

Betty's Do-Ahead

Brimming with apples, this moist cake is almost a pudding, and it becomes even more so when topped with the buttery sauce. You can bake the cake and prepare the sauce a day ahead and store them separately (refrigerate sauce). Warm the sauce in a saucepan over low heat, and heat individual pieces of cake uncovered in the microwave on High for 25 to 35 seconds or until warm.

Slow Cooker Pumpkin–Apple Dessert

Prep: 15 min **Cook:** 2 hr

(see photo insert)

1 can (21 ounces) apple pie filling

2 cups all-purpose flour

1 1/4 cups packed brown sugar

1 cup canned pumpkin (not pumpkin pie mix)

3/4 cup fat-free cholesterol-free egg product

1/3 cup vegetable oil

2 teaspoons baking powder

1 teaspoon ground cinnamon

1/2 teaspoon ground nutmeg

1/4 teaspoon baking soda

1 Spray 3 1/2- to 6-quart slow cooker with cooking spray. Spoon pie filling into cooker; spread evenly.

2 Beat remaining ingredients with electric mixer on low speed 1 minute, scraping bowl constantly. Beat on medium speed 2 minutes, scraping bowl occasionally. Pour batter over pie filling.

3 Cover and cook on high heat setting 1 hour 30 minutes to 2 hours or until toothpick inserted in center comes out clean.

1 Serving: Calories 260 (Calories from Fat 55); Fat 6g (Saturated 1g); Cholesterol 0mg; Sodium 140mg; Carbohydrate 50g (Dietary Fiber 2g); Protein 4g. **Diet Exchanges:** 1 Starch, 2 Fruit, 1 Fat.

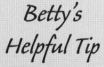

Betty's Helpful Tip

Check the cook times carefully. The smaller, more vertical slow cooker (3 1/2-quart size) will cook differently than a large, more horizontal cooker (6-quart size).

Harvest Upside-Down Cake

Prep: 15 min   **Bake:** 50 min

10 servings

1/3 cup butter or
margarine

1/2 cup packed brown
sugar

2 medium cooking apples,
peeled and sliced

1/2 cup whole berry
cranberry sauce

1 1/3 cups all-purpose
flour

1 cup granulated sugar

2 teaspoons baking
powder

1/2 teaspoon salt

1/3 cup butter or
margarine, softened

2/3 cup milk

1 teaspoon vanilla

1 egg

1 Heat oven to 350°. Melt 1/3 cup butter in heavy 10-inch ovenproof skillet or square pan, 9 × 9 × 2 inches, in oven. Sprinkle brown sugar evenly over butter. Arrange apple slices in row around edge of skillet. Arrange remaining slices in 2 more rows in skillet. Spoon cranberry sauce between rows.

2 Mix flour, granulated sugar, baking powder and salt in large bowl. Add 1/3 cup butter, milk and vanilla. Beat on medium speed 2 minutes, scraping bowl constantly. Add egg. Beat on medium speed 2 minutes, scraping bowl frequently. Pour over fruit in skillet.

3 Bake about 50 minutes or until toothpick inserted in center of cake comes out clean. Immediately place heatproof serving plate upside down onto skillet; turn plate and skillet over. Leave skillet over cake a few minutes (brown sugar mixture will run down over cake); remove skillet.

1 Serving: Calories 345 (Calories from Fat 115); Fat 13g (Saturated 8g); Cholesterol 55mg; Sodium 320mg; Carbohydrate 54g (Dietary Fiber 1g); Protein 3g. **Diet Exchanges:** Not Recommended.

Betty's Special Touch

Melt away the chill of late fall with this warm, homey dessert. Top with a dollop of sweetened whipped cream or a scoop of cinnamon ice cream.

Crimson Crumble Bars

Prep: 20 min   **Bake:** 32 min   **Cool:** 1 hr   **36 bars**

2 cups fresh or frozen cranberries

1 cup granulated sugar

2 teaspoons cornstarch

1 can (8 ounces) crushed pineapple in unsweetened juice, undrained

1 cup all-purpose flour

2/3 cup old-fashioned or quick-cooking oats

2/3 cup packed brown sugar

1/4 teaspoon salt

1/2 cup butter or margarine, cut into pieces

1/2 cup chopped pecans

1 Heat oven to 350°. Spray rectangular pan, 13 × 9 × 2 inches, with cooking spray. Mix cranberries, granulated sugar, cornstarch and pineapple in 2-quart saucepan. Heat to boiling, stirring frequently; reduce heat. Cover and simmer 10 to 15 minutes, stirring occasionally, until cranberries pop and sauce is translucent.

2 While fruit mixture is simmering, mix flour, oats, brown sugar and salt in large bowl. Cut in butter, using pastry blender or fork, until crumbly. Stir in pecans. Reserve 1 cup mixture for topping. Press remaining crumb mixture in pan.

3 Pour fruit mixture over crust. Sprinkle with reserved crumb mixture.

4 Bake 28 to 32 minutes or until top is golden brown. Cool completely on wire rack, at least 1 hour. For bars, cut into 6 rows by 6 rows.

1 Bar: Calories 100 (Calories from Fat 35); Fat 4g (Saturated 1g); Cholesterol 0mg; Sodium 45mg; Carbohydrate 15g (Dietary Fiber 1g); Protein 1g. **Diet Exchanges:** 1 Fruit, 1 Fat.

Betty's Helpful Tip

Packages of cranberries freeze well in their original plastic bags. The berries don't need to be thawed before use, but they should be rinsed in cool water.

White Chocolate Chunk–Cranberry Cookies

Prep: 15 min   **Bake:** 12 min per sheet   **Cool:** 32 min   **About 5 1/2 dozen cookies**

2/3 cup packed brown sugar

1/2 cup granulated sugar

1/2 cup butter or margarine, softened

2/3 cup shortening

1 teaspoon vanilla

1 teaspoon finely shredded orange peel

1 egg

2 1/4 cups all-purpose flour

1 teaspoon baking soda

1/4 teaspoon salt

2/3 cup dried cranberries

1 package (6 ounces) white baking bars (white chocolate), cut into 1/4- to 1/2-inch chunks

White Chocolate Glaze (below)

1 Heat oven to 350°. Beat sugars, butter, shortening, vanilla, orange peel and egg in large bowl with electric mixer on medium speed until light and fluffy, or mix with spoon. Stir in flour, baking soda and salt. Stir in cranberries and white baking bar chunks.

2 Drop by rounded teaspoonfuls about 2 inches apart onto ungreased cookie sheet.

3 Bake 10 to 12 minutes or until light brown. Cool 1 to 2 minutes; remove from cookie sheet to wire rack. Cool completely, about 30 minutes. Drizzle with White Chocolate Glaze.

1 Cookie: Calories 90 (Calories from Fat 45); Fat 5g (Saturated 2g); Cholesterol 10mg; Sodium 45mg; Carbohydrate 11g (Dietary Fiber 0g); Protein 1g. **Diet Exchanges:** 1 Fruit, 1 Fat.

White Chocolate Glaze

1 package (6 ounces) white baking bars (white chocolate), chopped

2 teaspoons shortening

Place ingredients in 2-cup microwavable measuring cup or deep bowl. Microwave uncovered on High 45 seconds; stir.

Betty's Special Touch

Instead of drizzling the glaze over the cookies, dip half of each cookie into the glaze. Or dip half of the cookies in the white chocolate glaze, and dip the other half in a semisweet chocolate glaze.

Spicy Pumpkin Drop Cookies

Prep: 15 min   **Bake:** 10 min   **Makes about 4 dozen cookies**

1 cup sugar

1/2 cup butter or margarine, softened

1 cup canned pumpkin (not pumpkin pie mix)

2 eggs

2 cups all-purpose flour

2 teaspoons baking powder

2 teaspoons ground cinnamon

1/2 teaspoon ground nutmeg

1/2 teaspoon ground ginger

1/4 teaspoon ground cloves

1 cup raisins, dried cranberries or dates

1/2 cup chopped nuts, if desired

1 Heat oven to 375°. Beat sugar and butter in large bowl with electric mixer on medium speed until light and fluffy, or mix with spoon. Beat in pumpkin and eggs. Stir in remaining ingredients except raisins and nuts. Stir in raisins and nuts.

2 Drop dough by rounded teaspoonfuls about 2 inches apart onto ungreased cookie sheet. Bake 8 to 10 minutes or until edges are set. Immediately remove from cookie sheet to wire rack.

---

1 Cookie: Calories 70 (Calories from Fat 20); Fat 2g (Saturated 1g); Cholesterol 15mg; Sodium 35mg; Carbohydrate 11g (Dietary Fiber 1g); Protein 1g. **Diet Exchanges:** 1/2 Starch, 1/2 Fruit.

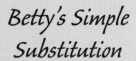

Betty's Simple Substitution

If you like oatmeal, make this old-time family favorite even more appealing by using 1/2 cup old-fashioned oats in place of 1/2 cup of the flour, and try dried cherries in place of the raisins.

Sweet Potato–Mallow Bars

Prep: 20 min   **Bake:** 46 min   **Cool:** 1 hr   **32 bars**

1/2 cup butter or
margarine, softened

3/4 cup packed brown
sugar

1 cup all-purpose flour

1/4 cup butter or
margarine, softened

1 cup packed brown
sugar

1 1/2 cups all-purpose
flour

1/2 cup sweetened
condensed milk

1 teaspoon
ground allspice

1 teaspoon
ground cinnamon

1 teaspoon orange
extract

1/4 teaspoon salt

1 egg

1 can (18 ounces)
vacuum-pack sweet
potatoes, drained
(1 cup)

3/4 cup chopped pecans,
if desired

Marshmallow Frosting
(below)

1 Heat oven to 350°. Grease bottom and sides of rectangular pan, 13 × 9 × 2 inches, with shortening; lightly flour. Beat 1/2 cup butter and 3/4 cup brown sugar in small bowl with electric mixer on medium speed until fluffy. Beat in 1 cup flour on low speed. Press in pan. Bake 10 to 13 minutes or until light golden.

2 Beat 1/4 cup butter and 1 cup brown sugar in large bowl on medium speed until fluffy. Beat in remaining ingredients except pecans and Marshmallow Frosting on low speed. Pour over crust. Sprinkle with pecans; press lightly.

3 Bake 29 to 33 minutes or until set. Cool completely, about 1 hour. Frost with Marshmallow Frosting. For bars, cut into 8 rows by 4 rows, using hot, slightly damp knife. Store covered in refrigerator.

1 Bar: Calories 180 (Calories from Fat 45); Fat 5g (Saturated 3g); Cholesterol 20mg; Sodium 75mg; Carbohydrate 32g (Dietary Fiber 1g); Protein 2g. **Diet Exchanges:** 1 Starch, 1 Fruit, 1 Fat.

Betty's Special Touch

Thanksgiving's favorite marshmallow-topped sweet potato casserole has been transformed into a delicious bar! If you choose not to use the pecans, lightly sprinkle top with a little cinnamon or pumpkin pie spice.

Marshmallow Frosting

1/2 cup light corn syrup

1 cup marshmallow
creme

2 egg whites

1/2 teaspoon cream of
tartar

1/4 teaspoon ground
cinnamon, if desired

Place corn syrup in small microwavable bowl. Microwave uncovered on High 1 to 2 minutes or until boiling. Stir in marshmallow creme. Beat egg whites, cream of tartar and cinnamon in medium bowl on high speed until soft peaks form. Beat in marshmallow mixture; continue beating on medium speed until stiff peaks form.

Slow Cooker Maple-Sauced Pears

Prep: 10 min   **Cook:** 2 hr 30 min   **Finish:** 10 min   **6 servings**

6 pears

1/4 cup packed brown sugar

2 tablespoons maple-flavored syrup or honey

1 tablespoon butter or margarine, melted

1 teaspoon orange peel

1/8 teaspoon ground ginger

2 teaspoons cornstarch

1 tablespoon orange juice

1 Peel pears. Core pears from bottom, leaving stems attached. Place pears upright in 3 1/2- to 5-quart slow cooker.

2 Mix remaining ingredients except cornstarch and orange juice; pour over pears.

3 Cover and cook on high heat setting 2 hours to 2 hours 30 minutes or until tender.

4 Remove pears from cooker; place upright in serving dish or individual dessert dishes.

5 Mix cornstarch and orange juice; stir into sauce in cooker. Cover and cook on high heat setting about 10 minutes or until sauce is thickened. Spoon sauce over pears.

1 Serving: Calories 180 (Calories from Fat 35); Fat 4g (Saturated 2g); Cholesterol 10mg; Sodium 30mg; Carbohydrate 35g (Dietary Fiber 3g); Protein 1g. **Diet Exchanges:** 2 Fruit, 1 Fat.

Betty's Special Touch

Serve an elegant dessert! Place each pear upright on a pretty dessert plate. Spoon sauce around pears, and sprinkle with chopped toasted nuts or coconut. Dollop a bit of soft whipped cream beside pears, and garnish the plate with a twisted orange slice.

Cranberry Mousse

Prep: 15 min   **Chill:** 2 hr 30 min   **6 servings**

1 1/2 cups cranberry-raspberry juice

3/4 cup sugar

3 tablespoons cornstarch

1/2 cup cranberry-orange sauce (from 12-ounce tub), thawed if frozen

1 cup whipping (heavy) cream

1 Heat cranberry-raspberry juice, sugar and cornstarch to boiling in 1-quart saucepan over medium-low heat, stirring frequently. Cook 1 minute. Stir in cranberry-orange sauce. Pour into medium bowl. Place plastic wrap directly on surface of mixture; refrigerate about 2 hours or until chilled.

2 Beat whipping cream in chilled small bowl with electric mixer on high speed until soft peaks form.

3 Stir chilled cranberry-raspberry mixture with wire whisk until smooth. Fold whipped cream into mixture. Spoon into 6 dessert dishes. Refrigerate about 30 minutes or until set.

1 Serving: Calories 310 (Calories from Fat 110); Fat 12g (Saturated 8g); Cholesterol 45mg; Sodium 20mg; Carbohydrate 49g (Dietary Fiber 1g); Protein 1g. **Diet Exchanges:** 3 Fruit, 3 Fat.

Cranberry Herbal Tea Granita

Prep: 15 min   **Freeze:** 5 hr   **Stand:** 20 min   **8 servings**

5 whole cloves

1 slice orange

2 cups water

1/2 cup sugar

1 stick cinnamon

3 tea bags red zesty herbal tea flavored with hibiscus, rose hips and lemongrass

1 1/2 cups cranberry juice cocktail

1 1/2 cups pineapple juice

Fresh fruit, if desired

Thin almond wafer cookies, if desired

1 Insert cloves into peel of orange slice. Heat water, sugar, cinnamon and orange slice to boiling in 2-quart saucepan, stirring occasionally; remove from heat. Add tea bags; cover and let steep 5 minutes. Remove tea bags, cinnamon stick and orange slice.

2 Stir cranberry and pineapple juices into tea. Pour into 2-quart nonmetal bowl or square baking dish, 8 × 8 × 2 inches. Cover and freeze about 2 hours or until partially frozen. Stir with fork or wire whisk. Cover and freeze 3 hours or overnight.

3 Remove granita from freezer 20 minutes before serving. Scrape surface with fork and spoon into glasses. Garnish with fruit and cookies.

1 Serving: Calories 145 (Calories from Fat 0); Fat 0g (Saturated 0g); Cholesterol 0mg; Sodium 5mg; Potassium 110mg; Carbohydrate 36g (Dietary Fiber 0g); Protein 0g. **Diet Exchanges:** 2 1/2 Fruit.

Betty's Special Touch

This refreshing dessert is the perfect light ending to a hearty meal. It looks prettiest served in wineglasses or small glass bowls.

Chocolate Truffle Brownie Cups

Prep: 15 min   **Bake:** 22 min   **Cool:** 40 min   **Stand:** 15 min   **48 brownie cups**

1 package (19.8 ounces) fudge brownie mix

1/4 cup water

1/2 cup vegetable oil

2 eggs

2/3 cup whipping (heavy) cream

6 ounces semisweet baking chocolate, chopped

Chocolate sprinkles, if desired

1 Heat oven to 350°. Place miniature paper baking cup in each of 48 small muffin cups, 1 3/4 × 1 inch.

2 Stir brownie mix, water, oil and eggs until well blended. Fill muffin cups about 3/4 full (about 1 tablespoon each) with batter. Bake 20 to 22 minutes or until toothpick inserted into edge of brownie comes out clean. Cool 10 minutes before removing from pan. Cool completely, about 30 minutes.

3 Heat whipping cream in 1-quart saucepan over low heat just until hot but not boiling; remove from heat. Stir in chocolate until melted. Let stand about 15 minutes or until mixture coats spoon. (It will become firmer the longer it cools.) Spoon about 2 teaspoons chocolate mixture over each brownie. Sprinkle with chocolate sprinkles.

1 Truffle Cup: Calories 80 (Calories from Fat 45); Fat 5g (Saturated 2g); Cholesterol 15mg; Sodium 5g; Carbohydrate 9g (Dietary Fiber 1g); Protein 1g. **Diet Exchanges:** 1/2 Starch, 1 Fat.

Betty's Do-Ahead

Bake and freeze unfrosted brownie cups for up to 1 month. Thaw brownie cups at room temperature before spooning glaze over them.

Super-Simple Menu

Serves 4 to 8

If this is the first Thanksgiving dinner you are preparing, or if you do not consider yourself an experienced cook but you'd like to try it anyway, start small. Consider purchasing dinner rolls and pie from your favorite bakery, or bake cookies or bars for dessert. Also, take up any offers of help from family or friends to round out your meal.

> *Butter- and Wine-Basted Turkey Breast,*
> *page 35*
> *Turkey Gravy (from a jar)*
> *Easy Mashed Potato Casserole, page 72*
> *Purchased Dinner Rolls*
> *Classic Cranberry Sauce, page 59*
> *Lime, Pineapple and Carrot Salad, page 139*
> *Impossibly Easy Pumpkin Pie, page 157*
> *or Spicy Pumpkin Drop Cookies, page 174*
> *Coffee and Tea*

Timing Countdown

2 or 3 days before dinner
- Buy groceries.
- Make Classic Cranberry Sauce; cover and refrigerate.

1 day before dinner
- Thaw turkey breast, if frozen, in refrigerator (see Thawing Your Turkey, page 14).
- Prepare Easy Mashed Potato Casserole up to the point of baking; cover and refrigerate.
- Make Lime, Pineapple and Carrot Salad; cover and refrigerate.

Morning of the dinner
- Bake Impossibly Easy Pumpkin Pie; cover and refrigerate. Or bake Spicy Pumpkin Drop Cookies; cover and keep at room temperature.
- Select serving dishes and utensils and set the table.

3 hours before dinner
- Wash turkey; pat dry with paper towels. Place turkey in oven for roasting.

35 minutes before dinner
- Remove mashed potatoes from the refrigerator and bake.
- Place cranberry sauce on table.

20 minutes before dinner
- Take turkey out of the oven; place on carving board or platter and cover with aluminum foil to keep warm.
- Place rolls in aluminum foil in oven to heat.
- Heat purchased gravy.
- Carve the turkey and arrange on a platter.

10 minutes before dinner
- Fill water glasses.
- Remove rolls from oven, and put in serving basket.
- Place gravy in serving bowl.
- Place the food on the table.

After Dinner
- Turn on coffee maker and/or make tea.
- Clear the table.
- Serve dessert.
- Serve coffee and tea.

Timesaving Today Menu

Serves 6 to 8

If saving time is your game, try high-heat roasting your turkey. Not only will it save you time, but your turkey will be beautifully and evenly browned, moist and tender, and there will be lots of drippings for homemade gravy. It's a huge help to prepare a side dish (potatoes) and bake biscuits and one dessert the day before. If your oven is large enough, you may be able to bake the biscuits while the turkey is roasting.

> *High-Heat Roast Turkey, page 24*
> *Milk Gravy, page 50*
> *Mushroom Stuffing, page 52*
> *Do-Ahead Mashed Potatoes, page 71*
> *Oven-Roasted Sweet Potatoes, page 78*
> *Classic Green Bean Casserole, page 69*
> *Cranberry-Orange Relish, page 61*
> *Angel Biscuits, page 120*
> *Pear-Cranberry Crisp, page 166*
> *Slow Cooker Pumpkin-Apple Dessert, page 170*
> *Wine, Coffee and Tea*

Timing Countdown

2 or 3 days before dinner

- Buy groceries.
- Make Cranberry-Orange Relish; cover and refrigerate.
- Make Angel Biscuits; cover and freeze.
- Thaw turkey, if frozen, in refrigerator (see Thawing Your Turkey, page 14).

1 day before dinner

- Prepare Do-Ahead Mashed Potatoes; cover and refrigerate.
- Prepare Mushroom Stuffing; cover and refrigerate immediately. **Don't stuff the turkey ahead of time.**
- Chill the wine.
- Select serving dishes and utensils and set the table.

Morning of the dinner

- Take biscuits out of freezer; let thaw at room temperature.

2 1/2 hours before dinner

- Wash turkey; pat dry with paper towels. Stuff turkey.
- Place turkey in oven for roasting immediately after stuffing.

2 hours before dinner

- Begin Slow Cooker Pumpkin-Apple Dessert.
- Prepare sweet potatoes for baking.

1 1/2 hours before dinner

- Place sweet potatoes in oven for roasting.

45 minutes before dinner

- Assemble Pear-Cranberry Crisp.
- Assemble Classic Green Bean Casserole.

35 minutes before dinner

- Take turkey out of the oven; place on carving board or platter and cover with aluminum foil to keep warm.
- Remove sweet potatoes from oven; keep warm by covering with aluminum foil.
- Lower oven temperature to 375°; place Green Bean Casserole and Pear-Cranberry Crisp in oven to bake.
- Remove stuffing from turkey; place in serving bowl and cover with aluminum foil to keep warm.
- Make Milk Gravy.
- Place biscuits in aluminum foil in oven to heat.
- Carve the turkey and arrange on a platter.

10 minutes before dinner

- Reheat mashed potatoes on high in microwave oven 4 to 5 minutes; stir before serving.
- Fill water glasses and serve wine.
- Remove biscuits from oven, and put in basket.
- Place gravy in serving bowl.
- Place the food on the table.

After dinner

- Turn on coffee maker and/or make tea.
- Clear the table.
- Serve desserts.
- Serve coffee and tea.

continues

My First Thanksgiving Dinner

Serves 8

This menu is for a traditional Thanksgiving dinner with all the trimmings. It isn't difficult, but it does take some planning. Make as much as possible ahead of time. Enlist other family members to help, buy items at the deli or bakery and take guests up on their offer to bring something, such as an appetizer or a bottle of wine.

> *Savory Pecans, page 128*
> *So-Simple Cranberry Gelatin Salad, page 137*
> *Classic Roast Turkey, page 18*
> *with Classic Bread Stuffing, page 52*
> *Classic Pan Gravy, page 48*
> *Do-Ahead Mashed Potatoes, page 71*
> *Classic Sweet Potatoes with Marshmallows, page 75*
> *Classic Cranberry Sauce, page 59*
> *Purchased Dinner Rolls*
> *Classic Pumpkin Pie, page 154*
> *Classic Apple Pie, page 161*
> *Wine, Coffee and Tea*

Timing Countdown

2 or 3 days before dinner

- Buy groceries.
- Thaw turkey, if frozen, in refrigerator (see Thawing Your Turkey, page 14).
- Wrap dinner rolls in aluminum foil and freeze to keep them fresh.
- Make Classic Cranberry Sauce; cover and refrigerate.
- Make Spiced Cream Clouds for Classic Pumpkin Pie and freeze.

1 day before dinner

- Bake Classic Pumpkin Pie and Classic Apple Pie; cover and refrigerate.
- Make Savory Pecans; cover tightly and leave at room temperature.
- Make Classic Bread Stuffing; cover and refrigerate immediately. **Don't stuff the turkey ahead of time.**

- Prepare Do-Ahead Mashed Potatoes up to the point of baking; cover and refrigerate.
- Make So-Simple Cranberry Gelatin Salad; cover and refrigerate.
- Cook sweet potatoes. Peel; cover and refrigerate.
- Chill the wine.
- Select serving dishes and utensils and set the table.

Morning of the dinner

- Take rolls out of freezer; let thaw at room temperature.

5 hours before dinner

- Wash turkey; pat dry with paper towels. Stuff with Classic Bread Stuffing.
- Place turkey in oven for roasting immediately after stuffing.

1 hour before dinner

- Set butter and cranberry sauce on the table.

45 minutes before dinner

- Remove mashed potatoes from the refrigerator and bake.
- Assemble sweet potatoes with marshmallows in baking dish.
- Set out bowl of nuts.

30 minutes before dinner

- Take turkey out of the oven; place on carving board or platter and cover with aluminum foil to keep warm.
- Place sweet potatoes with marshmallows in oven.
- Place rolls in aluminum foil in oven to heat.
- Remove stuffing from turkey; place in serving bowl and cover with aluminum foil to keep warm.
- Make Classic Pan Gravy.
- Carve the turkey and arrange on a platter.

10 minutes before dinner

- Fill water glasses and serve wine.
- Remove rolls from oven, and put in serving basket.
- Place gravy in serving bowl.
- Place the food on the table.

After dinner

- Turn on coffee maker and/or make tea.
- Clear the table.
- Cut the pies; serve on small plates. Top pumpkin pie with Spiced Cream Clouds.
- Serve coffee and tea.

Thanksgiving Dinner for a Crowd

Serves 20

It's easiest to serve a large number of people buffet style, so set everything up on a large table or kitchen counter, and let guests help themselves. If you are serving more than 20, these recipes can easily be doubled.

> *Ham with Zesty Cranberry Sauce, page 95*
> *High-Heat Roast Turkey, page 24*
> *Classic Pan Gravy, page 48*
> *Layered Vegetable Salad, page 140*
> *Slow Cooker Chorizo, Pecan and Cheddar Stuffing, page 56*
> *Easy Mashed Potato Casserole, page 72*
> *Bread Machine Blueberry Corn Bread, page 113*
> *Spicy Fruit Compote, page 63*
> *Classic Sweet Potatoes with Marshmallows, page 75*
> *Classic Baked Corn Pudding, page 83*
> *No-Crust Harvest Pumpkin Pie, page 156*
> *Orchard Squares, page 164*
> *Coffee and Tea*

Timing Countdown

3 days before dinner
- Buy groceries.
- Thaw turkey, if frozen, in refrigerator (see Thawing Your Turkey, page 14).
- Prepare Bread Machine Blueberry Corn Bread; cool and slice. Wrap in aluminum foil and freeze to keep fresh.
- Make Spicy Fruit Compote; cover and refrigerate.

2 days before dinner
- Cook sweet potatoes. Peel; cover and refrigerate.

1 day before dinner
- Bake No-Crust Harvest Pumpkin Pie and Orchard Squares; cover and refrigerate.
- Prepare Easy Mashed Potato Casserole up to the point of baking; cover and refrigerate.
- Bake the ham and make Zesty Cranberry Sauce; cover and refrigerate.

- Make Layered Vegetable Salad; cover and refrigerate.
- Select serving dishes and utensils and set the table.

Morning of the dinner
- Make Slow Cooker Chorizo, Pecan and Cheddar Stuffing; cover and refrigerate.
- Take rolls or bread out of freezer; let thaw at room temperature.

3 1/2 hours before dinner
- Place stuffing in slow cooker for cooking.
- Wash turkey; pat dry with paper towels. Place turkey in oven for roasting.

2 hours before dinner
- Carve ham; cover and refrigerate.
- Prepare Classic Baked Corn Pudding.

1 hour before dinner
- Set butter and Spicy Fruit Compote on the table.

45 minutes before dinner
- Assemble Sweet Potatoes with Marshmallows in baking dish.

30 minutes before dinner
- Take turkey out of the oven; place on carving board or platter and cover with aluminum foil to keep warm.
- Place Sweet Potatoes with Marshmallows in oven.
- Place rolls in aluminum foil in oven to heat.
- Make gravy; keep warm.
- Carve the turkey and arrange on a platter.

10 minutes before dinner
- Remove mashed potatoes from the refrigerator and heat in microwave oven.
- Remove ham and sauce from refrigerator.
- Remove bread from oven, and put in serving basket.
- Place stuffing in serving bowl or serve from slow cooker.
- Place stuffing in serving bowl.
- Place gravy in serving bowl.
- Place the food on the counter or table.

After dinner
- Turn on coffee maker and/or make tea.
- Clear the table.
- Cut No-Crust Harvest Pumpkin Pie and Orchard Squares; serve on small plates.

Helpful Nutrition and Cooking Information

Nutrition Guidelines

We provide nutrition information for each recipe that includes calories, fat, cholesterol, sodium, carbohydrate, fiber and protein. Individual food choices can be based on this information.

Recommended intake for a daily diet of 2,000 calories as set by the Food and Drug Administration

Total Fat	Less than 65g
Saturated Fat	Less than 20g
Cholesterol	Less than 300mg
Sodium	Less than 2,400mg
Total Carbohydrate	300g
Dietary Fiber	25g

Criteria Used for Calculating Nutrition Information

- The first ingredient was used wherever a choice is given (such as 1/3 cup sour cream or plain yogurt).
- The first ingredient amount was used wherever a range is given (such as 3- to 3 1/2-pound cut-up broiler-fryer chicken).
- The first serving number was used wherever a range is given (such as 4 to 6 servings).
- "If desired" ingredients and recipe variations were not included (such as sprinkle with brown sugar, if desired).
- Only the amount of a marinade or frying oil that is estimated to be absorbed by the food during preparation or cooking was calculated.

Ingredients Used in Recipe Testing and Nutrition Calculations

- Ingredients used for testing represent those that the majority of consumers use in their homes: large eggs, 2% milk, 80%-lean ground beef, canned ready-to-use chicken broth and vegetable oil spread containing not less than 65% fat.
- Fat-free, low-fat or low-sodium products were not used, unless otherwise indicated.
- Solid vegetable shortening (not butter, margarine, non-stick cooking sprays or vegetable oil spread as they can cause sticking problems) was used to grease pans, unless otherwise indicated.

Equipment Used in Recipe Testing

We use equipment for testing that the majority of consumers use in their homes. If a specific piece of equipment (such as a wire whisk) is necessary for recipe success, it is listed in the recipe.

- Cookware and bakeware without nonstick coatings were used, unless otherwise indicated.
- No dark-colored, black or insulated bakeware was used.
- When a pan is specified in a recipe, a metal pan was used; a baking dish or pie plate means ovenproof glass was used.
- An electric hand mixer was used for mixing only when mixer speeds are specified in the recipe directions. When a mixer speed is not given, a spoon or fork was used.

Cooking Terms Glossary

Beat: Mix ingredients vigorously with spoon, fork, wire whisk, hand beater or electric mixer until smooth and uniform.

Boil: Heat liquid until bubbles rise continuously and break on the surface and steam is given off. For rolling boil, the bubbles form rapidly.

Chop: Cut into coarse or fine irregular pieces with a knife, food chopper, blender or food processor.

Cube: Cut into squares 1/2 inch or larger.

Dice: Cut into squares smaller than 1/2 inch.

Grate: Cut into tiny particles using small rough holes of grater (citrus peel or chocolate).

Grease: Rub the inside surface of a pan with shortening, using pastry brush, piece of waxed paper or paper towel, to prevent food from sticking during baking (as for some casseroles).

Julienne: Cut into thin, matchlike strips, using knife or food processor (vegetables, fruits, meats).

Mix: Combine ingredients in any way that distributes them evenly.

Sauté: Cook foods in hot oil or margarine over medium-high heat with frequent tossing and turning motion.

Shred: Cut into long thin pieces by rubbing food across the holes of a shredder, as for cheese, or by using a knife to slice very thinly, as for cabbage.

Simmer: Cook in liquid just below the boiling point on top of the stove; usually after reducing heat from a boil. Bubbles will rise slowly and break just below the surface.

Stir: Mix ingredients until uniform consistency. Stir once in a while for stirring occasionally, often for stirring frequently and continuously for stirring constantly.

Toss: Tumble ingredients (such as green salad) lightly with a lifting motion, usually to coat evenly or mix with another food.

Metric Conversion Guide

Volume

U.S. Units	Canadian Metric	Australian Metric
1/4 teaspoon	1 mL	1 ml
1/2 teaspoon	2 mL	2 ml
1 teaspoon	5 mL	5 ml
1 tablespoon	15 mL	20 ml
1/4 cup	50 mL	60 ml
1/3 cup	75 mL	80 ml
1/2 cup	125 mL	125 ml
2/3 cup	150 mL	170 ml
3/4 cup	175 mL	190 ml
1 cup	250 mL	250 ml
1 quart	1 liter	1 liter
1 1/2 quarts	1.5 liters	1.5 liters
2 quarts	2 liters	2 liters
2 1/2 quarts	2.5 liters	2.5 liters
3 quarts	3 liters	3 liters
4 quarts	4 liters	4 liters

Weight

U.S. Units	Canadian Metric	Australian Metric
1 ounce	30 grams	30 grams
2 ounces	55 grams	60 grams
3 ounces	85 grams	90 grams
4 ounces (1/4 pound)	115 grams	125 grams
8 ounces (1/2 pound)	225 grams	225 grams
16 ounces (1 pound)	455 grams	500 grams
1 pound	455 grams	1/2 kilogram

Measurements

Inches	Centimeters
1	2.5
2	5.0
3	7.5
4	10.0
5	12.5
6	15.0
7	17.5
8	20.5
9	23.0
10	25.5
11	28.0
12	30.5
13	33.0

Temperatures

Fahrenheit	Celsius
32°	0°
212°	100°
250°	120°
275°	140°
300°	150°
325°	160°
350°	180°
375°	190°
400°	200°
425°	220°
450°	230°
475°	240°
500°	260°

Note: The recipes in this cookbook have not been developed or tested using metric measures. When converting recipes to metric, some variations in quality may be noted.

Index

Complete your cookbook library with these *Betty Crocker* titles:

Betty Crocker's Best Bread Machine Cookbook
Betty Crocker's Best Chicken Cookbook
Betty Crocker's Best Christmas Cookbook
Betty Crocker's Best of Baking
Betty Crocker's Best of Healthy and Hearty Cooking
Betty Crocker's Best-Loved Recipes
Betty Crocker's Bisquick® Cookbook
Betty Crocker's Bread Machine Cookbook
Betty Crocker's Cook It Quick
Betty Crocker's Cookbook, 9th Edition— *The* **BIG RED** *Cookbook*®
Betty Crocker's Cookbook, Bridal Edition
Betty Crocker's Cookie Book
Betty Crocker's Cooking Basics
Betty Crocker's Cooking for Two
Betty Crocker's Cooky Book, Facsimile Edition
Betty Crocker's Diabetes Cookbook
Betty Crocker's Easy Slow Cooker Dinners
Betty Crocker's Eat and Lose Weight
Betty Crocker's Entertaining Basics
Betty Crocker's Flavors of Home
Betty Crocker's Great Grilling
Betty Crocker's Healthy New Choices
Betty Crocker's Indian Home Cooking
Betty Crocker's Italian Cooking
Betty Crocker's Kids Cook!
Betty Crocker's Kitchen Library
Betty Crocker's Living with Cancer Cookbook
Betty Crocker's Low-Fat Low-Cholesterol Cooking Today
Betty Crocker's New Cake Decorating
Betty Crocker's New Chinese Cookbook
Betty Crocker's A Passion for Pasta
Betty Crocker's Picture Cook Book, Facsimile Edition
Betty Crocker's Quick & Easy Cookbook
Betty Crocker's Slow Cooker Cookbook
Betty Crocker's Southwest Cooking
Betty Crocker's Ultimate Cake Mix Cookbook
Betty Crocker's Vegetarian Cooking